THE
GREATNESS
OF OUR GOD

THE
GREATNESS
OF OUR GOD

DISCOVERING THE TRUE NATURE
OF THE GOD OF GLORY

HUGH BARBER

To order additional copies of this book, contact:
Xlibris Corporation
1-800-618-969
www.Xlibris.com.au
Orders@Xlibris.com.au
501512

CONTENTS

Great is the LORD and most worthy of praise; his greatness no one can fathom. One generation will commend your works to another; they will tell of your mighty acts . . . The LORD is gracious and compassionate, slow to anger and rich in love. The LORD is good to all; he has compassion on all he has made . . . The LORD is faithful to all his promises, and loving toward all he has made.

Psalm 145:3-4; 8-9; 13 NIV

ACKNOWLEDGEMENTS

My many thanks and gratitude to my family and friends who have made me the person I am today. Thank you mum for giving me your incredible determination and endless love. Dad for your encouragement and great humour.

Thank you to my local church, *C3 Oxford Falls* and all the pastors who have been faithful to their calling. Your incredible examples of what it means to be followers of Christ have made a deep impact on my life.

Specific thanks to the men and women of God who have inspired me to rise up and be a man of faith, conviction and example to others: Pastors Phil & Christine Pringle, Mark & Bernie Kelsey, Pat & Amanda Antcliff, Mark Saundercock, Mike Cooney and others . . .

My deepest thanks also to my good friends and counselors who have stuck by me over the years: Drew Castle, Joel McMahon, Carene Krishnan, Matt Anderson, Chris Pace, Ed Worrall and many others. Thanks especially to Steve McAnally for the awesome design of the book, legend!

Most importantly, thank you to my God, Jesus Christ and the Holy Spirit who have been faithful to me from the beginning of my walk with Him at seventeen. Only He truly knows how far I have come and the personal battles I had to overcome. Thank you for giving me the privilege and opportunity to write this book and trusting me with this message. To God be the Glory forever and ever.

Hugh Barber
Northern Beaches, Sydney

INTRODUCTION

The idea of this book came during a men's bible study I lead on Monday nights. After prayer one afternoon on the beach, the idea to study the nature of God gave me the inspiration to teach on it as a seven part series. It was a huge success which brought rich understanding to all of us. Some nights the studies just left all of us totally speechless. Immediately I thought to myself—*others need to hear this too* . . .

After much observation, study and reflection, I came to the conclusion that the majority of people do not understand the true nature of God. Many today have an incorrect and twisted opinion of God. Their life experiences determine if God is either good or bad. After getting past the first hurdle that *Yes, He does exist*, in their thinking He is either one extreme of 'angry and vengeful', or the other extreme of 'love and grace'. Sometimes people think He is a mixture of both at different times and can't make up His mind!

In reality it is the enemy who has worked overtime in distorting the true nature of God. Words of lies have become beliefs and strongholds in the minds of many. They falsely believe God is absent, demanding, hard to please, and many more. These beliefs sadly keep many away from discovering the truth that He is in actual fact a Great God. That all those who choose to live for Him serve a good and happy God who He delights in. I am convinced if our foundation in God's nature is strong, when the storms of life come we will never doubt His goodness in their purpose and how to come out of them better for it.

I believe that a thorough and deep understanding of the fundamental nature of God is essential for every individual to discover for themselves. This book will cover the following characteristics of God and their important contemporaries:

Mercy/Judgement, Goodness/Destruction, Grace/Cursing's, Love/Wrath, Peace/ Anxiety, Faithfulness/Rejection and Abundance/Poverty.

While I will never say I have discovered everything there is to know about the nature of God, I believe that this book is a good foundation into relating to the Greatness of our God, who can never be completely known by any man. I believe this book has the potential to unlock your relationship with your Heavenly Father, and captivate you and your love and respect for Him to a whole new level. It is my conviction that we need to know the nature of God *now* more than ever before. It is this revelation and understanding that will keep us in the faith during the hard times, and on the path of eternal life. The nature of God tells us that we are here for something so much greater than what the world tells us. That *He* is the reason for our existence and there is a divine calling for every individual to discover for themselves.

Personally, this book has also been the result of many years of discoveries, trials and victories of God slowly revealing Himself to me. It is my prayer that God will reveal Himself to you in a whole new way, and will be the start of a brand new journey, as you discover for yourself—**The Greatness of our God!**

~ SECTION ONE ~

CHAPTER 1

The Greatness of our God

When you understand the character of a person, you will understand
their choices and decisions in life. God is no different—when we
understand His divine character and nature, we will agree and
appreciate His decisions and judgements for our lives as well.

How awesome is the LORD Most High,
the Great King over all the earth!
—Psalm 47:2 NIV

Is Greatness Attainable?

The word 'Greatness' stirs up many emotions and imaginations. Every person
desires to be great or achieve some level of greatness in their chosen field. Greatness
comes on many levels and many capacities. In most cultures, it is reserved for only
the famous and highly favoured, the elite and the powerful.

One definition of greatness includes *the state, condition, or quality of being great;*
greatness of size, mind, power.[1] The word has many meanings, including magnitude
in size, significance in prominence, or renown for excellence, fame or impressiveness.
Nouns include outstanding in character and reputation, someone of great importance,
superior in nature, noble, powerful and influential. Antonyms include insignificance,
irrelevance, ordinary and trivial.

Greatness is a concept heavily dependent on a person's perspective and biases. Whether someone or something is Great or not depends from subjective judgements of the value of one person or thing as compared to another.

—Webster's Dictionary

The title of greatness is given to people in history who have brought radical social reforms in the midst of injustice. Soldiers at war who performed incredible acts of bravery. And leaders of nations who changed history by their example of convictions and integrity. William Shakespeare perhaps best summed it up best: '*Some are born great, some achieve greatness and some have greatness thrust upon them*'.

Some of my favourite sporting legends who have achieved greatness in their chosen arena include Roger Federer, Cristiano Ronaldo, Darryn Lockyer and Sachin Tendulkar. Their reputations precede them wherever they travel, and their presence carries great authority and respect. Other favourite business professionals include Richard Branson, Warren Buffet, James Cameron and JK Rowling. Their influence and legacy in their industries is truly inspiring.

However, I propose that the greatness of man is contradictory in some respect. Even some of the greatest of men and women would admit that they would not call themselves 'Great', knowing best their limitations and weaknesses. No one is perfect and very few can forever live up to the standards and expectations of the public eye, fanfare and industry critics. Furthermore, some former 'Great' athletes who broke world records are later found out to be drug cheats or living a highly scandalous double life.

Inventors of ground breaking discoveries are often ignored by the busyness of life. Entrepreneurs of global franchises soon become obsolete, with the speed of technology advancing at a rapid rate. And let's not forget—no one remembers who received runner up.

Human nature is flawed and always prone to choose evil over good. The most popular words in the English language are 'Me', 'I' and 'Want'. Everything we do since birth is totally dominated by self. Our happiness is dependant on these three words. At times we will stop at nothing to get what we want, when we want it, and how we want it. But it never satisfies. We are never content and feel complete. For instance, a child is never taught to lie when caught doing wrong, steal cookies from the kitchen and scream when they don't get their way immediately. Their most common words are 'Mine', 'I' and 'No', often in tears at a high pitched scream. Sharing with others is painful and there is never enough presents they can receive at Christmas. Just throw a chocolate amongst a classroom of children and you will see human nature at its worst!

According to William Hazlitt, a 19th century English writer, *'No really great man ever thought himself so'*. History has shown that even the greatest of men have fallen from grace. Man is tempted by specifically three things: Lust, Money and Power. Our human nature craves pleasure, greed and pride. Any of these in even a small dose has the potential to derail a person's character and bring much destruction to themselves and others. Ultimately, our sinful nature is to do evil until we eventually destroy ourselves. Now that we have established this definition and paradox, let us now ask a timely question . . .

Disbelief in God during times of Skepticism

We live in a highly diverse world of beliefs and with many options to choose from. Some of the top religions in the world today include: Christianity (all denominations), Islam (Shiite and Sunni), Buddhism, Hinduism, Judaism, primal indigenous and Chinese traditional (Asia, Africa, Americas). Additionally, though not a religion but a movement, is secular non-religious atheism. This movement has grown in size and influence significantly in recent years. It has been well known in its communication against the belief in God and outright skepticism at religion and faith altogether.

Well known atheists Richard Dawkins and Christopher Hitchens have inspired the masses to turn away from traditional faiths, with their views on 'the God factor'. In his book *The God Delusion* (2006), Dawkins argues a supernatural creator almost certainly does not exist and that religious faith is a 'delusion'. He does not claim to 'disprove God' with absolute certainty but suggests evolution is a 'simpler explanation'. Interestingly, though the book was popular, it provoked widespread negative responses from not only religious but atheist commentators and critics.[2]

Oxford University professor Alistair McGrath wrote *The Dawkins Delusion* (2007) in response. He says Dawkins ignorance of religion and specifically Christian theology makes him unable to engage religion and faith intelligently. His views are especially anti-religious, and do not allow his ideas to be examined or challenged. He objects to Dawkins' assertion that faith is a 'juvenile delusion', arguing that numerous reasonable persons choose to convert as adults, including scientists. To argue that all life was a matter of evolution involving chance and luck, is a hollow argument for even the simple minded. Atheism says, in no uncertain terms, 'you are an accident, have no purpose being here, and when you die you will go nowhere'. Hardly inspiring or helpful in a world full of unprecedented pain, worry, hopelessness and violence.

Atheism is a strange idea. Even the devil and his angels never fell for that vice.
—Charles Spurgeon, British Baptist preacher (1834-1892)

Another example of disbelief in God is the late Christopher Hitchens book *God Is Not Great: The Case Against Religion* (2007). Hitchens argues organised religion is violent, irrational, intolerant, allied to racism, tribalism, bigotry, and invested in ignorance. He believes people can be good without God with morality, and spends much time criticising religion, especially Christianity.

However, morality is ambiguous and different to everyone. What is acceptable to one person is unacceptable to another. Morality is subjective. Why then do people steal, rape, murder and commit crimes against humanity? What is clear from human history is how moral collapse most always follows spiritual collapse. In reply to Hitchens criticism of the bible, Will Hamblin, a professor at Brigham Young University said:

It is quite clear that Hitchens's understanding of biblical studies is flawed at best. He consistently misrepresents what the Bible has to say, fails to contextualise biblical narratives in their original historical settings, implies unanimity among biblical scholars on quite controversial positions, and fails to provide any evidence for alternative scholarly positions, or even to acknowledge that such positions exist at all . . . . His musings on such matters should not be taken seriously, and should certainly not be seen as reasonable grounds for rejecting belief in God.[3]

Coincidently, his brother Peter Hitchens, a former militant-atheist now Christian, wrote *The Rage Against God* (2010) in response. He argues that his brother's verdict on religion is misguided, and that faith in God is both a safeguard against the collapse of civilisation into moral chaos, with particular reference to events which occurred in the Soviet Union. He uses many examples of ordinary and famous people whose lives have been turned around by a physical experience of an encounter with God. It is clear that the evidence of a changed life is the greatest proof of a very real and living God.

Christianity is a faith of *radical transformation*. It is not a religion that makes you a better person by the accumulation of knowledge, good deeds or reaching a point of 'enlightenment'. It is a gospel of personal transformation of a life turned around when correctly applied. Most other religions focus predominantly on self and efforts to get right with their 'god'. However, Christianity says you are already made right through Jesus Christ and His sacrifice in our place on the Cross. No other person in history has been able to rise from the dead unassisted after being dead for three days. If someone can medically die and come back to life that is good enough evidence to say they are God.

Personally, after reading Christopher Hitchens book *God Is Not Great*, I was deeply saddened. Not for the title or the content of the book as much, but by the example of men and women, from namely Abrahamic religions, who have so badly misrepresented the One Great God they proclaim to serve. *Religious people* who profess to a faith of a God of love, and instead of doing good have destroyed countless lives. *Religious people* who have acted hypocritical and abused their positions of power. *Religious people* who have emphasised violence and hatred in order to achieve 'holy' and self-centered outcomes.

This book is not in any means an attack at either Dawkins or Hitchens. I refuse to waste time in senseless debates and conflict over differing life experiences and beliefs. Hitchens book, in fact, has a lot of truth of the evils of religion when used for selfish purposes. But what is not true is the God written of behind these faiths. He has been misrepresented by people who do not know Him. For if they knew Him they would live and act in a way that reflects His true nature.

This book is a case for the Greatness of God from a Christian perspective. Who He really is regardless of fallen man's attempts to follow and imitate Him. He has been misrepresented and misinterpreted for far too long. Now that we have this understanding clear, let us now ask possibly the biggest and most important question any person can ever ask . . .

Is God Really Great?

> *I know that the LORD is great, that our Lord is greater than all gods.*
> *The LORD does whatever pleases him, in the heavens and on the earth,*
> *in the seas and all their depths.*
> —Psalm 135:5-6 NIV

The author of Psalm 135 had a revelation of the Greatness of God. It was not a theology or a theory; it was a *personal encounter* with God himself. That He is the *greatest* of all the gods, both real and imagined. Despite beliefs that God is somehow 'a figment of our imagination', in reality He is actively involved in our everyday lives. He is as real and alive as life itself. He is whoever you need Him to be: A Healer. A Father. A Provider. Or a Friend. His significance is as great as the air that we breathe as He is the source of all life. We need Him every moment of every hour of every day. But He draws near to only those who draw near to Him.

Man has made up many 'gods' from his imagination, either due to superstition, good intentions or passed down traditions. There is only one true LORD. All other gods are inferior or insignificant. He is the creator of Heaven and Earth, the Great *Yahweh*, *Jehovah* and *Elohim*; ancient Hebrew names not to be applied to any false god. He is supreme over all things. *For the LORD is the great God, the great King above all gods* (Psalm 95:3).

He is a Great King far above all that is worshipped as gods, or to whom homage is paid. If the sun, the moon, or the stars were worshipped, if the mountains or the rivers, or angels good and bad, yet Yahweh is above all these. Yahweh in his perfections is exalted far above all that is ascribed to them, for He is the true God, and the Ruler of the universe.[4]

In His sovereignty God does whatever He pleases. But in everything He does it is best and good. He can do no evil for His character is flawless. He simply doesn't know any other way. He created life and people purely for relationship and intimacy. Nothing is missed or unknown to Him. Every activity in heaven and on earth is observed and recorded. He is *omnipresent*: everywhere at every time. *Omnipotent*: infinitely all powerful, able to do all things within the confines of His nature. And *omniscient*: has all understanding and knowledge, fully aware of all things actual and possible from the microscopic to the infinite in every realm at all times. He has no beginning and no end.

Psalm 47:2 says, *How awesome is the LORD Most High, the Great King over all the earth!* He is the Great King over all the earth. His title as King deserves full honour, value and respect. But how often do we treat Him as something much less? Like a cleaner, street sweeper or a genie in a lamp with three wishes in our time of need? Though He would have every right for us to tremble in fear and bow down, this is not His way. His ways are higher than our ways. Often we are guilty of being too smart for our own good, thinking our thoughts are better than God's and believing our ways are superior to His ways. Only to find out we were completely wrong and for our lives to fall apart. Truth doesn't change truth. God still remains God even if we think otherwise.

The Heavens Declare the Glory of God

The Heavens proclaim the glory of God. The skies display his craftsmanship.
Day after day they continue to speak; night after night they make Him known.
They speak without a sound or word; their voice is never heard. Yet their message
has gone throughout the earth, and their words to all the world.
—Psalm 19:1-4 NLT

Every person sees with their own eyes every day the beauty of creation. Only a blind person can be excused of not acknowledging the Greatness of the Creator. When you see an artwork you see the mind of the artist. Likewise when you see creation you see into the mind of the Creator. Regardless if you live in the African desert, the Swiss Alps, the Amazon rainforest in Brazil, or the Northern Beaches in Sydney, Australia, creation speaks of the Greatness of God. It sounds like a contradiction but it isn't. Creation speaks but does not say a word. Its silent messages speak of beauty, detail and extravagance.

The fact that we are alive on this planet is truly incredible. No other life form has ever been found with such perfect conditions for humanity to exist. The earth's solar system perfectly rotates around our sun providing twelve hours of sunlight, and our moon providing light twelve hours at night. If the earth was to be any closer to the sun it would be too hot for life to exist, and any further away too cold to be sustainable. Surely if we were to even catch a glimpse of how it was all created, we would be overwhelmed by its shear detail! To see creation is to see the mind and the heart of the Creator.

He alone has spread out the heavens and marches on the waves
of the sea. He made all the stars—the Bear and Orion, the Pleiades
and the constellations of the southern sky. He does great things too
marvelous to understand. He performs countless miracles.
—Job 9:8-9 NLT, author's emphasis

When I was in High School, I had the privilege to travel overseas for three weeks with a group of students to trek the Inca Trail in South America. I distinctly remember being personally touched by the geography and landscape upon miles and miles of scenery everyday. Each morning I would wake up, pause and think to myself that there has to be more to this life than me. There must be a Designer who made what I'm seeing and experiencing right now. One of my favourite down times is watching captivating sunrises in the morning and clear night time skies at night. This reminds me that I am not the centre of the universe. I am minuscule in comparison to all of creation, yet out of everything He made, *I* am His masterpiece.

Natural Revelation Theory says God reveals Himself through nature. By simple observation that we live in a world of remarkable beauty, variety, colour and abundance is enough evidence in itself of God's existence. Any sunrise or sunset is a pleasure to the eyes and a marvel to behold. Every person around the world has the opportunity to experience the delights of eating wholesome foods, and see the complexities of animals and insects. To know the joys of wonderful relationships and experience the incredible fulfillment of living our dreams and doing the desires of our hearts. And all of this was no accident. It was deliberately thought out and planned by the Greatness of the Creator. Scripture confirms this:

> *Great is the LORD and most worthy of praise; his greatness no one can fathom.*
> *One generation will commend your works to another; they will tell of your might*
> *acts . . . The LORD is gracious and compassionate, slow to anger and rich in love.*
> *The LORD is good to all; he has compassion on all he has made . . . The LORD is*
> *faithful to all his promises, and loving toward all he has made.*
> —Psalm 145:3-4; 8-9; 13 NIV, author's emphasis

This is possibly one of the most powerful statements written in the Bible about God Himself. The psalmist declares His Greatness which is worthy of our individual praise. This does not sound at all like a suggestion or careless thought, but a *revelation* beyond understanding. His Greatness is beyond our understanding. No wonder people are so confused about God!

Every generation in human history without realising has publically praised His creation. Further on the psalmist declares because of this, mankind is privileged to daily enjoy its benefits at no cost. He is truly *gracious and compassionate, slow to anger and rich in love*. He has no favorites' or partiality—He is good to all people—the rich or poor, the sick or healthy, the forgotten or the famous. His creation is evidence that He is loving to all He has made. Oh, the Greatness of our Creator!

But how can we know for sure that God is Great? Even in our moments of doubt and lack of faith, as we often are, what rock solid proof do we have that God is Good let alone Great? Let's look no further than the account of creation.

The Story of Creation

In the beginning God created the heavens and the earth. The earth was formless and empty, and darkness covered the deep waters. And the Spirit of God was hovering over the surface of the waters. Then God said, "Let there be light," and there was light. <u>And God saw that the light was good</u> . . . Then God said, "Let there be a space between the waters, to separate the waters of the heavens from the waters of the earth." And that is what happened. God made this space to separate the waters of the earth from the waters of the heavens . . . Then God said, "Let the waters beneath the sky flow together into one place, so dry ground may appear." And that is what happened. God called the dry ground "land" and the waters "seas." <u>And God saw that it was good</u>. Then God said, "Let the land sprout with vegetation—every sort of seed-bearing plant, and trees that grow seed-bearing fruit. These seeds will then produce the kinds of plants and trees from which they came." . . . <u>And God saw that it was good</u>. Then God said, "Let lights appear in the sky to separate the day from the night. Let them mark off the seasons, days, and years . . . <u>And God saw that it was good</u>. Then God said, "Let the waters swarm with fish and other life. Let the skies be filled with birds of every kind." . . . <u>And God saw that it was good</u> . . . Then God said, "Let the earth produce every sort of animal, each producing offspring of the same kind—livestock, small animals that scurry along the ground, and wild animals." . . . <u>And God saw that it was good</u>.
—Genesis 1:1-25 NLT, author's emphasis

We must not go any further until we understand the original intent of God in everything He created. In the creation account we see very clearly that everything God created was 'good'. Nothing was done with flaws, mistakes, errors or imprecision in His details in *all* of His creation. He created everything out of absoloutly nothing. Hebrews 11:3 says, *By faith we understand that the universe was formed at God's command, so that what is seen was not made out of what was visible.*

God is so powerful that the universe with all the stars, planets and galaxies was *spoken* into existence. The earth and all the billions or species of plants, animals, insects down to the tiniest of molecules was created. Water for oceans was given boundaries. Animals were diverse and detailed in mammals and species. Plants and trees were comprehensive and beautiful in all shapes and sizes. Before Adam sinned, there was harmony and peace in every part of creation. Everything created operated in complete order, unity and perfection. Anything less is simply not His best!

There is no hint of self-centeredness or selfish motivation in creating the world and everything in it. God creates because God loves and shows His love in His creation—a world of life, perfection, detail, beauty and extravagance on every level. Before there was a choir to praise Him, God praised Himself. Before there was a psalmist to write about the Greatness of the Creator, He did not hold back and personally commend His own work. Everything He made was spoken into being; such is His power and authority. Creation was perfect and flawless in every way.

When Job questioned God and accused Him of wrongdoing at His sufferings, God silences him by simply arguing His Greatness as Creator of heaven and earth! *Who is this that questions my wisdom with such ignorant words? Brace yourself like a man, because I have some questions for you, and you must answer them. "Where were you when I laid the foundations of the earth? Tell me, if you know so much. Who determined its dimensions and stretched out the surveying line? What supports its foundations, and who laid its cornerstone as the morning stars sang together and all the angels shouted for joy? "Who kept the sea inside its boundaries as it burst from the womb, and as I clothed it with clouds and wrapped it in thick darkness? For I locked it behind barred gates, limiting its shores. I said, 'This far and no farther will you come. Here your proud waves must stop!'* (Job 38:1-11).

God's Masterpiece

The Genesis account of Creation ends on an interesting note: *Then God said, "Let us make human beings in our image, to be like us . . . Then God blessed them and said, "Be fruitful and multiply. Fill the earth and govern it. Reign over the fish in the sea, the birds in the sky, and all the animals that scurry along the ground"* (Genesis 1:26-28).

Finally, man was created last as a sign of the final touches, highlight and zenith of His creation. Everything God created was for our personal enjoyment. Every fresh piece of fruit tasted is a gift. Drinking chilled water on a hot day is a gift. The joy of embracing a distant close friend is a gift. The indescribable excitement of falling in love is a gift. He creates because He loves.

Paul confirms this in his letter to the Ephesian church: *For we are God's [own] handiwork (His workmanship), recreated in Christ Jesus, [born anew] that we may do those good works which God predestined (planned beforehand) for us [taking paths which He prepared ahead of time], that we should walk in them [living the good life which He prearranged and made ready for us to live]* (2:10). Before time began, there God knew you and dreamed about you. He planned for you to do good works and to walk in His ways. Amazing!

It almost sounds too good to be true. *You* are the finest masterpiece of God's entire creation! *You* are the finishing touches of His work. *You* are everything He desired. What's more in the age to come everything God has is yours for Eternity as an heir in Christ. Romans 8:17 says *Now if we are children, then we are heirs—heirs of God and co-heirs with Christ, if indeed we share in his sufferings in order that we may also share in his glory.*

This includes all the galaxies, stars, planets, solar systems and all of the riches and glory of the Kingdom of Heaven. Ultimately though He created you for intimacy and relationship. An eternal relationship that will never end. For good measure, let's now look at four areas that prove beyond all doubt God's Greatness.

1) God is Great Because God is Good

> *Know that the LORD, He is God;*
> *It is He who has made us, and not we ourselves;*
> *We are His people and the sheep of His pasture . . .*
> *For the LORD is good; His mercy is everlasting,*
> *And His truth endures to all generations.*
> —Psalms 100:3; 5 NKJV

Here we see mankind is not robots, slaves or 'things', but *His people*. Like the sheep of His pasture, we have value, worth, significance. As our chief Shepherd, He desires to protect us, feed us and lead us into places of abundance and goodness. Our role is to simply trust and obey, fully believing that He knows what's best for us.

God is Great because essentially He is the *definition* of everything that is Good. Man is a sinner so He provides us a Saviour. Man experiences sickness so He assumes the office of Healer. Man is by nature corrupted so He brings Redemption. Man needed rescuing so He offers us Salvation. Man is burdened with many worries, so He provides us Peace. Man is finite and will one day die, so God has made an Eternal dwelling for us!

Many doctors today are stunned of the multitude of health benefits from the Law of Moses given thousands of years before medicine and technology could identify what causes harmful germs and bacteria. The Law written approximately 1,450BC contains remarkable rules relating to public health, food contamination, sewage disposal, infectious diseases and health education.[5]

It should not surprise us that obedience to God's commandments and other laws would promote good health. When we obey them and co-operate in accordance with His instructions we will be healthy, happy and strong. As our Creator, He knows what's best for us. We serve a good God who knows exactly what we need in every circumstance. We will look more into this in chapter 4.

2) God is Great Because God is Love

> *This is how God showed his love among us: He sent his one and only Son into the world that we might live through him. <u>This is love: not that we loved God, but that he loved us and sent his Son as an atoning sacrifice for our sins.</u> Dear friends, since God so loved us, we also ought to love one another. No one has ever seen God; but if we love one another, God lives in us and his love is made complete in us.*
> —1 John 4:9-12 NLT, author's emphasis

Scripture clearly speaks of God's most striking manifestation as His love. Not with gifts and presents, but with the greatest gift of all; the gift of His son Jesus and His death on the Cross. God has exhibited His Greatness by paying the price of redemption Himself—the death of His only Son in our place of punishment.

For scripture to declare that '*God is Love*' is to say that He is the definition of Love. He is the definition of goodness. He is the definition of affection. Apart from Him we can not even begin to understand what true love is. A love that is unconditional, uncompromising and unbending at all times and all situations. A love that is never selfish or self-centered. A love that would lay down their life and die in our place if needs be. Even death on a cross . . .

God's Love is expressed greatest by giving mankind a second chance to be redeemed from eternal destruction. While we were His enemies, (being dead, wicked and guilty), Christ died willingly for us in our place (Romans 5:8, author's notes). Although no one can see God visibly here on earth, He can be seen through His followers who live radical lives for Him and reflect His nature (1 John 4:12). The apostle John clearly says that the greatest attribute of God living within us is *love*. To love those who offend us, to love our enemies, to love the unlovable. We will look more into this in chapter 6.

3) God is Great Because God is Light

> *This is the message which we have heard from Him and*
> *declare to you, that <u>God is light and in Him is no darkness</u> at all.*
> —1 John 1:5 NKJV, author's emphasis

Light represents what is good, true, wonderful and just. This is to say that God can never lie, manipulate or be guilty of evil. There is simply no trace of darkness in Him. He is the definition of everything that is good, true, happiness and delightful. In fact, God is absolutely perfect and there is nothing in Him which is in any way imperfect, or would blemish the pure splendor of His character; not even as much as the smallest spot would be seen on His white robes of Glory.[6]

This understanding brings new meaning to 1 Peter 2:9, *You have been called out of the darkness and into His wonderful light.* Darkness represents all types of evil and wickedness practiced and devised by man. Once when we lived in darkness and were a thousand miles from Him, He still desired relationship with us and called us by name out of our darkness and into His wonderful light. James 1:17 says, *Whatever is good and perfect comes down to us from God our Father, who created all the lights in the heavens. He never changes or casts a shifting shadow.*

For scripture to declare that God is light is to say that He is the complete definition of everything that is good and perfect. Apart from Him we can never understand what true goodness really is. In the dark, good and evil look the same, but when light is shined on both they are clearly distinguished. If God had ever changed we would have permission to doubt. Though we change and our opinions of God change every day, he never changes (Hebrews 13:8).

4) God is Great Because God is Perfect

> *Be perfect, therefore, as your heavenly Father is perfect.*
> —Matthew 5:48 NIV

True Greatness is ultimately perfection. Perfection is beyond our ability. Our fallen nature proves that pretty well. But perfection comes pretty easy to God. He is not a fault finding perfectionist. He already knows you and I are not perfect, so He provides mercy with every day (Lamentations 3:23)! The mystery of the perfect relationship of the Trinity allows God to be perfect. The Father, Son and Holy Spirit are all perfectly holy and submitted to one another. To be submitted is to completely serve one another sacrificially, willingly and cheerfully. The universe operates in complete order because of the accountability of this perfect relationship and understanding. This adds new meaning to the scripture: *By the mouth of two or three witnesses every word may be established* (Matthew 18:16). There is unity and truth when people come together in agreement.

All are One but have different roles. The Father speaks, Jesus does, the Holy Spirit reveals. God the Father spoke the universe into being. When Adam sinned and all dominion was given to Satan, God spoke again and prophesied his total defeat by Jesus on the Cross taking back the keys of Death and Hades. Genesis 3:15 says, . . . *he will crush your head, and you will strike his heel.*

When the right time came, God sent His own Son to earth, miraculously born of a virgin woman, fulfilling all the requirements under the law (Galatians 4:4). The gospels record that everything Jesus said and did was only what He saw the Father doing (John 5:19). Amazing! Jesus never once operated out of His own will. His will was the will of the Father, which was a blameless life free from all sin and deceitfulness. Adam's perfection was untested perfection. However, Jesus' perfection was tested and proved true.

Likewise, the Holy Spirit is the Spirit of Truth who comes down from Heaven. He marks us with a seal, a deposit guaranteeing our salvation (see Ephesians 1:13-14). A seal is attached to a letter to authenticate its authority. This seal distinguishes between what is genuine and what is a counterfeit. The Holy Spirit is the great change agent and transformer. He sanctifies us to become perfect, just as our Father is perfect.

Foundations of Righteousness and Justice

Righteousness and justice are the foundation of your throne;
love and faithfulness go before you.
<u>Blessed are those who have learned to acclaim you,</u>
<u>who walk in the light of your presence, LORD.</u>
They rejoice in your name all day long;
they celebrate your righteousness.
For you are their glory and strength . . .
—Psalms 89:14-17 NIV, author's emphasis

What an amazing statement! God is self-governed completely by the laws of the universe—divine Righteousness and Justice, but always done in love and faithfulness. God is Great because everything He does is founded on these two principles. Furthermore, He gives all people the opportunity to walk in His paths, and those that do He calls them blessed!

Righteousness and Justice are two sides of the same coin. If God is to continue being God, He can not simply set justice aside and sweep sin under the rug. He must deal with it decisively and with exacting justice. When God finally judges on the last day, not one sin will receive more punishment than it deserves, and not one good work will be forgotten or rewarded (see 2 Corinthians 5:10). Because He is the Judge of the Universe, every decision He makes is therefore completely divine, righteous and just. He judges according to His Eternal wisdom, seeing and knowing all events as they have already taken place.

Even though life is hard and at times unfair, God still remains Great. This is not to suggest that all evil comes directly from God. We must understand that we live in a fallen world and tragedies take place by either accident, misfortune or the enemy against our souls. However, we are encouraged to run to God who is our strong fortress, knowing that we are but strangers in this land and have an eternal dwelling place. We have a hope that all things work together for good, no matter how bad life gets. Because Christ suffered for us on the Cross, our suffering identifies with Him. God has good reasons for what He does do, and His answer to our suffering is comfort and healing is Himself.

Some suggest that because God is all powerful that surely He is guilty of slipping up somewhere in history, because power corrupts even the best of men. John Dalberg Acton, a 19th century historian, expressed this opinion in a letter in 1887, *'Power tends to corrupt, and absolute power corrupts absolutely. Great men are almost always bad men'*. This saying is a timeless truth and paradox to all mankind. The basic understanding of this phrase is that a person's sense of morality lessens as his or her power increases. How the more powerful a person becomes, the more they feel free to do whatever they want. Absolute power is a far more dangerous weapon than a nuclear bomb. It is the breeding ground for absolute corruption along with every crime imaginable.

However, this can not be true to God. Though He has all power and all control over all the stars, planets, galaxies, Heavens and Earth, power can not corrupt Him or tempt Him to do evil. God in His Greatness can never be accused of selfishness or wrongdoing, because that would be completely against His nature. It is simply impossible for Him to do anything sinful or evil, ever! Now that we have established this foundation of God's Greatness, let us now examine and look at the nature of the God of Glory.

CHAPTER 2

The Nature of God

God's nature is multi-faceted and all glorious; like a priceless diamond
with many faces, all wonderful and far too great for our minds to
comprehend.

*Christ walked with men on earth that He might show them what God is like and
make known the true nature of God to a race that had wrong ideas about Him.
This was only one of the things He did while here in the flesh, but this He did
with beautiful perfection. From Him we learn how God acts towards people. The
hypocritical [and] the basically insincere will find Him cold and aloof, as they once
found Jesus; but the penitent will find Him merciful; the self-condemned will find
Him generous and kind. To the frightened He is friendly, to the poor in spirit He is
forgiving, to the ignorant, considerate; to the weak, gentle; to the stranger, hospitable.*
—A.W Tozer, pastor and author (1897-1963)[1]

After much experience and study I have found that the majority of people
do not understand the true nature of God. Many today have an incorrect and
distorted picture of who God really is. The challenges and painful events of life
determine if God is good or bad to them. After getting past the first hurdle that
Yes, He does exist, in people's thinking He is either one extreme of 'always angry'
and impossible to please, or the other extreme of 'God is love' so I can live just
the way I like. Some people think God is a mixture of both at different times, in
addition to being distant and irrelevant to us today.

They think He is a mixture of both at different times and He can't make up His
mind, while believing that they have done God a favour by being 'nice' or simply

their existence! Some humorous views I have heard are: '*God is an anxious dictator sitting on a throne somewhere in space*'. Pacific Islander beliefs interpret weather patterns as a sign of His emotions—sunshine when happy, storms when angry. And, '*God has become obsolete after thousands of years and is irrelevant to today's 21ˢᵗ century? Let's just get on with our lives*'.

My view on the subject is more positive than negative. While I do accept both views on the Holiness and Judgement of God, my emphasis is more positive and swayed towards His Goodness to those who respond on His terms. That all those who choose to live for Him serve a good and happy God, who if we delight in, He will give us the desires of our hearts (Psalm 37:4).

Firstly, it is my conviction that we *can* know God, personally and powerfully. His nature is best represented as multi-faceted; like a priceless diamond with many faces, all wonderful and far too great for our minds to comprehend. Paul writes, *I will live in them and walk among them. I will be their God, and they will be my people* (2 Corinthians 6:16). It is assumed that if God promises us He will *live in us* and *walk among us*, that we would know His nature. We would love what He loves and hate what He hates.

One of the most amazing promises in scripture is if we draw near to God, He will draw near to us (James 4:8). This is an open invitation for everyone and anyone who desires to know God personally. It applies to all people, from all backgrounds, throughout all of human history—past, present, future. God is bound to His word. He will never lie and go back on what He has promised. It is clear: God is as real, alive and as close as you want Him to be.

Genesis 1:26 says, *Then God said, "Let us make human beings in our image, to be like us . . ."* His nature is everything people are except without the sinful nature. We by nature reflect Him in our emotions, feelings, heart, mind and spirit. Because of Adam's sin, the sinful nature entered into all humanity and we now possess the knowledge of good and evil. When we pass from this life to the next, our bodies will be glorified and we will become just like Him. 1 John 3:2 is our promise: *Beloved, now we are children of God; and it has not yet been revealed what we shall be, but we know that when He is revealed, we shall be like Him, for we shall see Him as He is.*

We are not an accident or product of coincidence billions of years in the making. We have a divine purpose being here; not just existing but living a life of fullness and relationship with our Maker. Out of the complete expression of His love He created us in the image of Himself; for us to know Him and to have deep relationship with Him. Truly God is good to all. He has revealed Himself and His grace to them. By His ways we may understand His precepts, the ways He requires us to walk in, and His promises and purposes.[2]

'In Love He Predestined Us . . .'

Praise be to the God and Father of our Lord Jesus Christ, who has blessed us in the heavenly realms with every spiritual blessing in Christ. For he chose us in him before the creation of the world to be holy and blameless in his sight. In love he predestined us to be adopted as his sons through Jesus Christ, in accordance with his pleasure and will to the praise of his glorious grace, which he has freely given us in the One he loves. In him we have redemption through his blood, the forgiveness of sins, in accordance with the riches of God's grace that he lavished on us with all wisdom and understanding.

—Ephesians 1:3-6 NIV, authors' emphasis

Wow! What a statement! You could camp on this passage for forty years and just meditate on its depth and significance. God is not so much our Creator or 'Master' we must obey, but our *Father*. In Christ is the key to access every blessing known to man. God desires to bless those He loves, and as a Father especially His children. And we are legally adopted into His family and receive our inheritance in Christ.

It is God's greatest pleasure for us to be called His sons and daughters. To have relationship with us and to reside in our hearts (see 1 John 4:12). We see from this passage again that God is Love. To those who think otherwise they have no idea how wrong they are. Scripture tells us that we are chosen since before the beginning of time to be holy and blameless in His sight. Just think about that for a moment. This is the highest call we can pursue. There is no greater pursuit in His eyes than for us to live in a way that honours and pleases Him. To be free from the corruptive influences of the world and free from sin entering our lives. The world today is anything but free because we have pursued the wrong things—to please self at the expense of all those around us. How far we have fallen from our true destiny.

The golden link between us and God is Jesus Christ. He is the perfect mediator between us and a Holy God. The path that we travel is the road of grace. His grace is freely and abundantly given to us. Like air we can only breathe in so much. You can never run out of air to breathe to remain alive. Likewise God's grace can never run out no matter how much we take. It is not just enough to get by—but rich and lavished! Though never to be abused or used improperly to live immoral lives.

God's wisdom is too great for us to fully comprehend and understand. In fact it is without measure. Psalm 147:5 says, *Great is our Lord, and mighty in power; His understanding is infinite.* And Isaiah 40:28, *Have you not known? Have you not heard? The everlasting God, the LORD, the Creator of the ends of the earth, neither faints nor is weary. His understanding is unsearchable.* His wisdom is so superior that there is no wisdom, no insight, no plan that can succeed against Him (Proverbs 21:30).

From this salvation through Christ, His greatest plan was the church. For believers to come together weekly in community and fellowship. To love and serve one another, making disciples spreading the amazing salvation that they have themselves have experienced. This was His *master plan* for you and me, predestined since the beginning of time. That the church would be an example of heaven on earth, whatever bound on earth is bound in heaven, and whatever loosed on earth shall be loosed in heaven (Matthew 18:18). We are living in the most exciting time in human history. A day is coming when the global church will be chief among the mountains of all influence, power and authority (Isaiah 2:2). A church Jesus spoke about. A church God dreamed about. The best is yet to come!

God's Nature is Determined by our Response to Him

> *Today I have given you <u>the choice between life and death</u>, between blessings*
> *and curses. Now I call on heaven and earth to witness the choice you make.*
> *Oh, that you would <u>choose life</u>, so that you and your descendants might live!*
> *You can make this choice by loving the Lord your God, obeying him,*
> *and committing yourself firmly to him. This is the key to your life.*
> —Deuteronomy 30:19-20 NLT, author's emphasis

Our decision to respond to God or not will have a significant effect on His nature towards us. Free will is to have complete control over our lives and therefore take personal responsibility to accept all consequences for our decisions and actions. Our free will is a gift from God to make everyday choices and what we want to do with our life. It is also the freedom to choose to live for ourselves or to live for God, to live for our kingdom or His Kingdom.

Deuteronomy 30 is clear that all people are given a choice. Love would not be complete if the object of someone's love was compelled or had no choice. The human will is one of the most powerful forces in the world. *Free will* is His way. God will never step over our final decisions at the end of the day.

When a gift is given freely and willingly, out of a joyful heart and spirit, it has great meaning and incredible worth. When done with complaining and grudgingly it effectively has zero value. This makes Christ's sacrifice on the cross so much more powerful. Scripture says, *For the joy set before Him He endured the cross* (Hebrews 12:2). On the way to the cross He was not bitter. Despite the pain and agony He went through, He never once complained. Jesus didn't once think, 'This is unbelievable! I've never once sinned and only loved people, performed miracles and taught them the Kingdom of God. This is the thanks I get?' No. He saw you and me being rescued from eternal separation to be saved from the penalty of our sins.

Ultimately our decision is to either choose Him or reject Him. In a democracy or republic people have many votes and options to choose from. But in God's

Kingdom, there is only one vote. There can be no middle ground. It is an *eternal* decision that can not be reversed. He demands our allegiance and loyalty, not religious duty to a set of rules. We are either hot or cold, committed or uncommitted, believers or pretenders.

This is why the writer pleads and beckons us to '*choose life!*' This is the key to your life and everything you need to have a blessed life. All we have to do is follow three simple commands: (i) Love God (ii) Obedience to His Ways, and (iii) Commitment to His Ways. And His commands are not difficult for us. *This is love for God: to obey his commands. And his commands are not burdensome* (1 John 5:3).

To Believe is to Obey

During my earlier years before I radically met Christ, I always called myself a Christian and believed in God. However, my life was full of selfishness, evil language, addictions and everything in between. I believed I was saved and heading to heaven but in reality my actions was in opposition to the very beliefs I claimed. I loved my sin and I owned my life, and no one was going to tell me how to live. Furthermore, I never attended church, read the Bible or only prayed when times got tough. My understanding of what it meant to be saved was narrow minded and deceived. It was only until a traumatic event from a broken long term relationship brought me to God, and I surrendered my life to Him for good. I was lost but now found. I was blind but now I see!

The most known passage John 3:16 says, *whoever believes in Him [Jesus Christ] should not perish but have eternal life*. The meaning of the word 'believe' many think all they are required to do is believe that Jesus existed and died on Calvary. That if they simply acknowledge His existence they are somehow in good standing with God. But this is far from the truth.

The root word of believe is to *obey*. Obedience is the greatest sign of a true believer. James makes this clear by saying: *But be <u>doers of the Word [obey the message]</u>, and not merely listeners to it, betraying yourselves [into deception by reasoning contrary to* *the Truth]. For if anyone only listens to the Word <u>without obeying</u> it and being a doer of it, he is like a man who looks carefully at his [own] natural face in a mirror; For he thoughtfully observes himself, and then goes off and promptly forgets what he was like* (1:22-24, author's emphasis).

Jesus Himself said, *If you love me, you will obey what I command* (John 14:15). Our faith is only as good as our obedience to His ways. The Pharisees were known as hypocrites because they outwardly professed a highly religious lifestyle, but in reality were full of pride and self-righteousness. When Jesus exposed them publically in order to protect their power they put Him on the Cross. They murdered the Son of God breaking all of their rules in the process!

Deuteronomy 30:20 says by choosing life you will commit yourself to *loving the Lord your God, obeying him, and committing yourself firmly to him.* Our obedience to this call is to receive all the promises of God and to have your eternal future secured. I implore you if you haven't already to choose God for yourself wholeheartedly. To live for Him and let Him be King over every area of your life. To live for something greater than yourself. There is nothing to lose but everything to gain. It's a good offer in my books—choose life!

Our Response is to Worship

> *Come, let us sing for joy to the LORD; let us shout aloud to the Rock of our salvation. Let us come before him with thanksgiving and extol him with music and song. <u>For the LORD is the great God, the great King above all gods</u> . . . <u>Come, let us bow down in worship, let us kneel before the LORD our Maker;</u> for he is our God and we are the people of his pasture, the flock under his care.*
> —Psalm 95:1-3; 6-7 NIV, author's emphasis

In every culture and community, music powerfully communicates current ideas, events and messages. It can motivate productivity in the workplace, inspire devotion to faith and prepare soldiers for war. Music stirs emotions, provokes our thoughts, and brings back memories. It is a powerful influencer, and speaks to the human heart like no other. Scientists have found that music stimulates more parts of the brain than any other human function. The power of music was recognised as far back as ancient civilisations. Today music is a multi-billion dollar industry. People love to listen to music of all genres, from rock to classical, jazz to heavy metal, and dance to inspirational.[3]

It is therefore no surprise that our response to the Greatness of God is to worship Him with music and song. God alone is worthy to receive our exclusive individual worship. The Greek word for worship is *proskuneo*. James Strong, an expert in interpretation of the bible, defines it as *to bow down, show reverence, to worship and adore*.[4] Worship can be expressed in many ways. Psalm 95 says our worship is to be vocal and expressed without restraint. He is worthy of our worship and our exclusive worship. Whatever we worship we give our whole heart to and draw our identity and strength from. It is whatever we gain our greatest meaning and value from.

However, the world has found many counterfeit forms of worship. Jack Frost's book *Spiritual Slavery to Spiritual Sonship* describes seven tendencies human nature is constantly drawn too and when solely pursued we ultimately worship. He calls these quite fittingly *counterfeit affections* which take the place over God:

1. **People**—the belief that a person is the answer to all your needs over God
2. **Passions**—anything which feeds the flesh and provides escapism, often taken in the form of addictions (alcohol, drugs, sexual immorality)
3. **Possessions**—thinking that what we own and possess will give us fulfillment through worldly gain
4. **Power**—a desire to control and have authority over others
5. **Place**—the belief that being somewhere or an environment will satisfy
6. **Performance**—a constant striving to accomplish and have achievement, strongly results dependent
7. **Positions**—the praise of man, determined to win the approval of others and having a title will make one happy.[5]

All of these are good in a sense and have value, but they are never to replace God in our lives. We are commanded to worship Him and to have no others as number one. He is a jealous God for our heart and devotion. He tolerates no rivals. Why? He loves us beyond our understanding, and love has no rivals. We become what we worship. When we worship money we become obsessed with greed. When we worship people we become obsessed with pleasing man. But when we worship God we become just like Him—Holy.

God is so amazing, so wonderful, so loving and so great, that He is *worthy* of our individual worship and life. We are told to bow down and kneel before Him—an act of surrender and submission to His authority and Lordship. If He is a Great King why would we worship anything less? This is the Greatness of our God!

> *All of God's acts are consistent with all of His attributes. No attribute contradicts another, but all harmonise and blend into each other in the infiniteness of all that He is. All that God does agrees with all that God is and always will be. His attributes explain and promote each other, giving us glimpses for the mind to meditate and enjoy over and over again*
> —A.W Tozer, pastor and author (1897-1963)[6]

All of Creation Worships God

I heard a funny story recently. Many years ago a popular Bible College student was awoken at 5:00 am in the morning by two native Kookaburra's singing as loud as possible right outside his bedroom window. Upset, he threw a shoe at them but missed. He then threw his other shoe and missed! So he went into the bathroom and started throwing his soap, toothbrush, toothpaste, shampoo and so on. Then the Holy Spirit spoke to him as clear as day and said, 'What are you doing? Who do you think they are singing too?'

If the birds and all of creation worships God, why would we not be an exception? When Jesus came into Jerusalem on a donkey and his followers began to shout and sing as they walked along, the Pharisees wanted them rebuked. But Jesus answered, *"I tell you, if these become silent, the stones will cry out!"* (Luke 19:40) It is improper for us to withhold worship from our Creator. The presence of God doesn't come with our hands in our pockets. We are to worship Him with our whole lives. In spirit and truth. To take up our Cross and follow His leading. To be living sacrifices as a sweet smelling aroma. Holy and set apart. A vessel of gold, ready for every good work. And to lay down our lives if necessary. Anything less is not our best.

Before I came to Christ I lived completely for myself—anything that made me happy and feel good. I was the king over my life and no one was going to tell me how to live. I was selfish in all of my ways and did everything for my own benefit. And like everyone else I looked to the world for my identity, worth and value. If I wore the latest clothes, styled my hair the right way and listened to the latest music I was 'cool'. If I spoke in a certain way and was up to date in all the latest movies and TV shows I was accepted. This meant acting in a certain way to fit in, even if it meant being someone I wasn't and didn't even enjoy it! However, I was still empty and wanting more. I was not satisfied. In reflection I was lost. It was not until I came to Christ that I got set free and realised how totally lost I was.

God's nature is multifaceted but always operating in complete harmony. Again, our response to Him largely dictates His nature towards us. When Moses gave Israel the final words before entering the Promised Land, he made it very clear that to choose to live for Him is to *choose life*. If you desire salvation He provides you a Saviour in Christ. From this decision, if you need healing He is your Healer. If you need protection He is your shield, fortress and stronghold. If you need provision, He will happily provide all of your needs. If you need a father, He adopts you as His child. If you need His forgiveness He forgives and justifies you in Christ. If you love Him He will love you. If you are faithful to Him He will be Faithful to you. God is whoever you need Him to be.

On the contrary, if you reject Him scripture says you have *chosen death*. This can come in a variety of ways which all end down a deadly path. If you choose to walk away He will let you. If you choose to live your life without God or love this world, you make yourself His enemy. If He asks you to do something that requires faithfulness and obedience and you are unfaithful and disobedient, your destination is ruin. And if you deny Him on earth He will deny you in Heaven.

God gives all people the choice to either choose eternity with Him or eternity without Him. This is a difficult but necessary truth. It is *essential* that we understand this correctly. God's nature towards us individually is determined by our response to Him. Every human being is given the option to make God Lord over their life or make themselves Lord, which is to choose life or death. I exhort you today if you haven't already—*choose life* so that you will live!

Jesus is Essential to Know God

Christ is the visible image of the invisible God. He existed before anything was created and is supreme over all creation, for through him God created everything in the heavenly realms and on earth. He made the things we can see and the things we can't see—such as thrones, kingdoms, rulers, and authorities in the unseen world. Everything was created through him and for him.
—Colossians 1:15-16 NLT

To understand the nature of God, we only have to look at His Son Jesus Christ. Colossians says *Christ is the visible image of the invisible God.* The word 'image' here is *eikon* meaning 'Christ is the exact copy, description and perfection of God Himself'.[7] This is one of the strongest statements about the divine nature of Christ found anywhere in the Bible. Jesus is not only equal to God, He is God and His life on earth fully revealed God to us (see John 10:30-38). When Isaiah prophesied the future Messiah 700 years before Christ he said, *Therefore the Lord Himself shall give you a sign: Behold, the young woman who is unmarried and a virgin shall conceive and bear a son, and shall call his name Immanuel [God with us].* (Isaiah 7:14, author's emphasis).

Jesus did not come to earth for His own purposes but was in fact sent by the Father. *Jesus said to them, If God were your Father, you would love Me and respect Me and welcome Me gladly, for I proceeded (came forth) from God [out of His very presence]. I did not even come on My own authority or of My own accord (as self-appointed);*

but He sent Me (John 8:42). One of the primary purposes God sent His Son was to show and teach us about Himself. Everything Jesus said and did was the exact representation of God's heart and nature. Every conversation Jesus had, every miracle He performed and every emotion He displayed. His heart for the lost and broken reflected God, just as His anger at hypocrisy and injustice reflected Him. It is essential that we see Christ accurately. When we see Christ we see the exact representation of the Father in His nature and character.

> *In the past God spoke to our ancestors through the prophets at many times and in various ways, but in these last days he has spoken to us by his Son, whom he appointed heir of all things, and through whom also he made the universe. The Son is the radiance of God's glory and the exact representation of his being, sustaining all things by his powerful word. After he had provided purification for sins, he sat down at the right hand of the Majesty in heaven.*
> —Hebrews 1:1-3 NIV, author's emphasis

Furthermore, no clearer evidence is required that God has spoken to us more loudly than the tangible presence of the Son Himself among us. In previous times, God spoke to people through prophets, in dreams, visions and nature. But just in case we were not listening, the Most High God sent His one and only Son from Heaven to Earth to make known His ways to mankind. Jesus is not only God but the exact representation and full expression of God in a human body. This is why Jesus could boldly say to the disciples, *He that has seen me has seen the Father* (John 14:9).

> *There is salvation in no one else! There is no other name in all of heaven for people to call on to save them.*
> —Acts 4:12 NLT

Jesus is sufficient to know God because through faith and obedience to Him is the only way to have access to the Father. The apostle John makes this clear when Jesus said, *I am the way, the truth and the life. No one can come to the Father except through Me* (John 14:6). Put simply, Jesus is *the method, the message* and *the meaning* of life. He is the tangible image of the invisible God. Some people complain that the way is too narrow for all to come to salvation. But thank God there is a way! What was impossible became possible. A God that was so far from us has now become so intimately close and within reach. To know and study the life of Jesus through history and the gospels is to know God Himself.

I have a feeling that God made it so simple so that as many people could come to Him as possible without hindrances. Both the educated and unlearned, the well and the broken and the great and the least of society. God deliberately chose the foolish things of this world to shame the wise:

> *Remember, dear brothers and sisters, that few of you were wise in the world's eyes or powerful or wealthy when God called you. Instead, God chose things the world considers foolish in order to shame those who think they are wise. And he chose things that are powerless to shame those who are powerful.*
> —1 Corinthians 1:27 NLT

Ultimately Jesus' sacrifice on the Cross was God's greatest act in history the world will ever know. It must be emphasised that *much* was achieved with Christ's work on the Cross that few really understand. It was at that moment the sins of the whole world by all people were paid for. The righteous took the place of the unrighteous. Perfection took the death penalty meant for the wicked. It was the *great exchange* that made the heavens and earth groan. The Cross is the epicenter and turning point of human history. It separated time from BC to AD. We are no longer under the old covenant of the Law but now under the new covenant of Grace. It is my firm conviction that we as individuals need to get back to the Cross. To know its *significance* and understand its *power* until it is a revelation we will never depart from.

Difficult Questions

Popular questions that I hear often are '*Who is God?*', '*How could God be Good?*', and '*How Could God be Great if there is so much evil in the world?*' I find these questions often come out of a place of ignorance. A favourite question I ask people is '*If God could do anything for you, what would you ask? If He has all power, all authority and all control over the Heavens and the Earth, what would you want?*' Regardless of the answer, I usually reply with, '*Well what have you done for Him lately?*' Too often, a lack of understanding of anything brings our own downfall. If we had the full picture and all the minute details, we would never be accused of assumptions ignorance. So why is the subject of God no different?

Scripture declares, *His ways are higher than our ways and His thoughts are greater than our thoughts* (Isaiah 55:8-9). No wonder so many miss God, because they don't understand His ways! Like trying to explain to a child the mechanics and engineering of a space ship, when they have just learnt their ABC's at the age of five. It is impossible to fully comprehend an infinite Creator. We need faith to believe He knows best for us. Yes, we can ask anything from Him and it is His good pleasure to give us what we pray for, on the condition that it is His will, it is a righteous request and asked for in faith without doubting (see John 14:12-16; 15:7; 16:22-23; 1 John 5:14-15).

Many people today believe their life is the centre of the universe. Self is King. I get what I want, when I want, how I want it. This is the most selfish and often depressing possible way to live. Life is not about what God can do for you, but what *you* can do for *Him*. In reality, God is the centre of the universe. He created us to please Him and have relationship in His presence. Not the other way round.

Again, free will accepts the fact that we have complete control over our lives and therefore accept all consequences for our decisions and actions. At the end of the day, God will give you exactly what you want. How often have we run off with our inheritance, full of vision and great ideas, only to waste it and destroy our lives? Could it be that we are wrong and He is right? He is waiting for us to come home to Him and be restored back into our rightful place (see Luke 15:11-32).

God's Nature is Revealed in God's Word

> *Your word is a lamp to guide my feet and a light for my path . . .*
> *Your laws are my treasure; they are my heart's delight.*

I am determined to keep your decrees, to the very end.
—Psalms 119:105; 111 NLT

We will understand God's nature when we understand His Word. The Bible is much more than a book of rules and laws and a list of do's and don'ts. Scripture is our roadmap to Heaven and our GPS system on how to get there. It is up to us to use it correctly and commit ourselves to studying it so we don't get lost. Scripture is our greatest authority and teaches us the nature and heart of God clearly and specifically. Many powerful leaders in history spoke highly of the Word of God in their lifetime:

It is impossible to rightly govern the world without God and the Bible.
—George Washington, 1st President of the United States (1732-1799)

The Bible is alive, it speaks to me; it has feet, it runs after me;
it has hands, it lays hold of me.
—Martin Luther, Father of Protestant Reformation (1483-1546)

The Bible is no mere book, but a Living Creature, with
a power that conquers all that oppose it.
—Napoleon, French Emperor (1769-1821)

2 Timothy 3:16-17 says *All scripture is inspired by God and is profitable, for teaching, rebuking, correcting and training in righteousness, so that the man of God may be thoroughly equipped for every good work.* All scripture is timeless and has direction for all people during all circumstances of life. In every season you can find an answer to every problem you are facing. From relationships to finances; making important decisions to even times of warfare.

Arguments that the Bible is outdated and irrelevant for today have no foundation. In all actuality it is one of the greatest and most trustworthy historical documents of all time. Having survived all attempts to have it removed from societies by rulers and dictators over hundreds of years, the Bible is still alive and well today. No other book has such unity and harmony despite being written by over forty authors from all walks of life over fifteen thousand years! While professors and academics love to regard themselves as knowing the truth and all the facts, it is the eternal Word of God that is the truth which surpasses all else, including people's thoughts and opinions.

Scripture is divinely inspired by God and His primary method for speaking to us to know His will for us today. This book will look at many passages of scripture as our primary source to discover a glimpse of the wonderful nature of God. Scripture has much to say about God's nature and His ways. I believe it was always His desire that we would take the initiative and to study and meditate His word so that we can be always pleasing to Him 2 Corinthians 5:9 says *Therefore, whether we are at home [on earth away from Him] or away from home [and with Him], we are constantly ambitious and strive earnestly to be pleasing to Him.* In the following chapters we will go deep into scripture and look at many verses to find the best conclusions of how we are to relate to our awesome God.

More importantly, scripture is to be our treasure and heart's delight. God's Word is literally words of life and food for our soul. It is our place of direction when we get lost and our path to stay on when there are many options to choose from. Within its pages are guidelines and commands for us to follow which are for our good and those around us. Every area of life is covered, from handling wealth and relationships to war and death, with practical wisdom—a timeless message for all generations.

> *Among its authors we find the tax-collector, the shepherd, fishermen, rich men, statesmen, preachers, exiles, captains, legislators, judges and, men of every grade and class. This wonderful volume is in reality a library, filled with history, genealogy, ethnology, law, ethics, prophecy, poetry, eloquence, medicine, sanitary science, political economy, and perfect rules for the conduct of personal and social life.*
> —H.L Hastings, English MP and writer (1833-1899)

Many sadly do not see the need to strictly adhere to all the commands of Christianity or think it is all too hard and brings no reward for their efforts.

In fact, the opposite is true. When you understand the purposes and the heart behind the rules, you no longer see the rules but the *person* behind them. For instance, when a parent gives rules and boundaries to their children, it is done in love to protect them and keep them from harm. They have their best interests at heart and see the bigger picture. A child that is given no direction for life and free reign will eventually become rebellious and out of control. They are given for their good, whether they understand or appreciate them or not.

The harsh truth is that the standards and laws of the world are very different to the ones God gave us to follow. It is fair to say that nine out of ten people's problems would be gone by simply conforming to the standards of God! Such rules as do not repay evil for evil, do not steal, envy, murder, commit adultery, forgive others as you have been forgiven, do to others as you would want them to do to you.. If we just obeyed them we would easily have half the problems the world is currently facing. These are far more than moral guidelines and good values—they come from the heart of our Creator who knows what will give us peace, joy, success and a long life in this challenging world.

If I were to take my car to the manufacturer I know that I can trust them when they give me advice on how to look after it. They took great lengths and effort to create my car, and they know how it runs inside and out, its strengths and abilities. How much more should we trust our Creator who made us, whom we are fearfully and wonderfully made? Since He knows us inside out, our human tendencies and abilities, surely we can trust Him with our lives. Let us never easily forget our Maker, Creator of heaven and earth.

I guarantee you that if people knew the true nature of God, they would reconsider their ways. To understand that we serve a God who is full of mercy and showers His goodness on all His creation. A God who is gracious to our failings and abounding in love towards His people. A God who promises peace to the soul and His faithfulness endures forever. And a God who is abundant and rich towards us, who desires for us to have life and to have it more abundantly. Any normal person who rejects this as evil, one would have to question his character and everything that he stands for. It is my conviction that we need to know the nature of God *now* more than ever before.

The Enemy Distorts the True Nature of God

Now the serpent was more crafty than any of the wild animals the LORD God had made. He said to the woman 'Did God really say . . . ?'

Genesis 3:1 NIV

The enemy has worked overtime throughout the centuries speaking lies about the true character of God. By perverting our perception of Him can easily make us draw away and lose heart when times get hard. But this should not be the case! If our foundation in God is strong, when the storms of life come we will never doubt God's purpose in using events to mature and strengthen us.

The devil has not changed since Adam and Eve in the Garden. He still uses the same tricks which are effective. By planting a seed of doubt about God's Word, we are very susceptible to take the bait and fall away. He did this in the garden with Eve when he asked her, *Did God really say, 'You must not eat from any tree in the garden?'* Here we see the devil at his best—the ultimate fault finder. In a world of perfection he speaks against the one rule given which was for their good. He is an anointed armchair critic, the worst of the worst.

The purpose of God giving man one law was to ensure He had *willing* children who obeyed Him out of love, not robots who had no other choice. By not placing a law there would be no option to disobey. The devil however, twisted God's commandment in order to attack and distort His character. By focusing on what Eve couldn't have, her focus completely forgot she could have everything else in the world! All of a sudden, bombarding thoughts came into her mind that God is withholding everything from her. Here we see a domino effect:

1) The enemy questions God's Word—His authority and its authenticity
2) This brings confusion over interpretation
3) Doubt over reliability and God's character sets in

4)   Instead of gratefulness in what has been given, there is now a focus on the one tiny exception of what we can't have.

Soon afterward, her eyes were staring at the fruit that only moments ago she wasn't even thinking about or had ever desired. Thoughts moved emotions, which moved a change of attitude that led to action. Desire set in and the rest is history. I often hear this voice when dreaming about my future. 'Did God really say your family will be saved?' 'I don't think you deserve that job'. The enemy also often attacks my convictions and knowledge of His Word. 'Does it really say He forgives *and* forgets all your sins? Why do you keep remembering them then?' 'Are you sure you're going to Heaven?'

Lies, lies, and more lies is the only weapon the devil has. Our response is Jesus' example—to fight him with the Word of God, a double edged sword. It is the sword of the Spirit which is the Word of God praying (Ephesians 6:17-18). I pray often when under spiritual attack, '*I bind you devil in the name of Jesus. You have nothing on me. I messed up today, but I've repented and now covered in the blood of Jesus. YOU messed up and there is no Saviour for you. Don't you dare remind me of my past because I will remind you of YOUR future—the Lake of Fire!*'

The correct rebuke from Eve should have been, "*Yes God DID say 'of every tree of the garden you may freely eat; but of the knowledge of good and evil you shall not eat'. I'll focus on what God has given me—everything in the world which He created for my personal enjoyment. I serve a good and wonderful God. Don't you dare try to change my mind devil, get behind me fat head!*"

The enemy still operates this way today. He portrays unjust leaders, bad fathers and dictators as the nature of God. Because they are authority figures it is easy to project their nature onto God's character since He is the ultimate authority. However, when you know God would *never* do anything to harm you, you will never second guess Him when tough times come. That whatever He does or does not do for you is ultimately in your best interests. He loves you and is the definition of love. He can never change for He is always unchanging. He sees what you can not see and is fighting your battles behind your back. He hears your every prayer which are in the process of being fulfilled. Faith says "I trust You even though I don't understand. I trust you even though I'm hurting right now".

Often children do not understand parent's reasons for withholding what they want. Self-centeredness causes us to be very shortsighted and unreasonable. They do not agree because of their immaturity. Likewise when we are truly lost in Jesus, we know everything He does is for our good. He looks at the eternal aspect of what we go through. In this understanding we can not be shaken or shipwrecked.

Before we go any further, we must first come to a place of humility and reverence that God is greater than we are. He is God and we are not. We must come to Him on His terms before we can ever assume to know any better. If we are to be accepted as the disobedient Prodigal Son was, we must come as he did—in deep repentance and honour. With this in mind, let's now look at a case study of the life of Moses and His experience with the Greatness of God.

Moses Knew the Nature of God

> *He revealed His <u>character</u> to Moses and His <u>deeds</u> to the people of Israel.*
> —Psalms 103:7 NLT, author's emphasis

When God called Moses to deliver the people of Israel out of slavery in Egypt, He first called them to Himself, not the Promised Land. There was no point transporting a nation of people accustomed to pagan worship and idolatry from one land to another, only for them to continue living in pagan worship and idolatry. Now, this generation saw more miraculous signs and wonders more than any other in history. They left Egypt with all their treasures and were delivered by an army without even a battle. Even in the harsh heat and climate of the Sinai desert, they were plentifully supplied water out of a rock and fresh bread from the heavens. A pillar of cloud even led them by hand through the day and a pillar of fire guided them through the night! But the best was yet to come—they were to encounter God themselves, the Creator of Heaven and Earth.

Moses experienced something few ever realise or understand its significance—He knew the *ways* of God. The word 'ways' here means His laws, methods of administration, the principles on which He governs mankind, and the conditions on which He will save people. There is no higher ground of gratitude to God than the simple fact that He has given a revelation of Himself to all mankind to know His wonderful ways.[8] Whereas the people of Israel knew only His acts and miracles, Moses had something far deeper and more valuable—a close relationship with God. From this relationship, God entrusted Moses to be the lawgiver for all humanity until Christ came to fulfill the law. His laws were His heart for His people. An expression of His heart to protect and bless all those who followed them faithfully.

God is so powerful that when He came to meet Moses and the nation of Israel, His seat was Mount Sinai! Being a mountainous area, His presence covered somewhere between a height of 2,600 metres and spanned several kilometers! His holiness was so great He commanded no living creature to be within certain boundaries of the mountain or they would surely die (see Exodus 19:9-13). Are you capturing a glimpse of the Greatness of our God?

The Ten Commandments—God's Heart for all People

God's law was first given to Moses who told the people of Israel. God's law represents a clear picture of God's nature and will for humanity. The Ten Commandments reflect a summary of standards He expected—people to God and people to people.

Let's look at one of the most significant events of Moses' life—experiencing the Greatness of God. Despite the restriction of who could draw near to God, Moses found favour with God and was given the honour to go up the mountain to talk to Him as a friend talks to a friend (Exodus 33:11). Moses was so close to relationship with God that he even dares to ask to see His glory. God simply replies, '. . . *but you may not look directly at my face, for no one may see me and live*' (Exodus 33:20). However, He allows Moses to see His back:

And the Lord passed by before him, and proclaimed, "The Lord! The Lord!
A God merciful and gracious, slow to anger, and abundant
in loving-kindness and truth . . ."
—Exodus 34:6 NIV, author's emphasis

This is one of the most powerful statements in the entire Bible. Here we see Moses has an encounter with the God of the Universe. His request was honest and genuine, to see the glory of God for himself with his own eyes. No other person in scripture records such a bold request. As the Lord passed by before him, I believe Moses was shouting at the top of his lungs, screaming and out of his mind in fact. *The Lord! The Lord! A God merciful and gracious, slow to anger, and abundant in loving-kindness and truth . . .*

Think about it: if you ever saw something remotely significant you would not be able to withhold your excitement and enthusiasm. This was Moses. I like the Message translation best: *God, God, a God of mercy and grace, endlessly patient—so much love, so deeply true—loyal in love for a thousand generations, forgiving iniquity, rebellion, and sin.*

Amazing! Do you really believe what you are reading? We serve an incredible God, full of mercy and grace, patient in our fallings and abundant in loving kindness and truth. Despite His Sovereignty and Holiness who has every reason to judge sin immediately so as to ensure universal justice is upheld, He withholds Himself because His mercy and grace are just as powerful. May we always meditate on the Greatness of our God.

When God reveals Himself to Moses, his revelation was six-fold! Firstly, when Moses saw God he shouted *"The Lord! The Lord!"* meaning he was likely shouting and intensely ecstatic and delirious that He was in the presence of the Most High, in all His Glory and Majesty. This sounds similar to Isaiah and John's experience (see Isaiah 6 and Revelation 4). Let us now look at how we should respond appropriately to the God of Glory.

Responding Appropriately

I beseech you therefore, brethren, by the mercies of God, that you <u>present your bodies</u>
<u>a living sacrifice, holy, acceptable to God,</u> which is your reasonable service.
—Romans 12:1 NKJV, author's emphasis

Where Moses *commanded* in the Old Testament under Law, Paul *pleaded* in the New under Grace. The work of the Cross achieved so much. The sins of the world have forever been dealt with. All people have to do is respond in genuine faith and obedience. Paul's argument is simple: because of His mercy we are to offer ourselves as living sacrifices. Daily sacrificing anything that can hinder your relationship with Him and sacrificing to strengthen your relationship with Him. We are to be holy which is to be set apart. A vessel of gold, ready for every good use (see 2 Timothy 2:20-21).

A form of worship is our life to become a living sacrifice. God expects our best sacrifices, reverence and worship. He is to be shown great reverence, honour and our best in everything we do. In the Old Testament, the worship His people brought them was in the form sacrifices of animals. But the worship we bring today is to be a living sacrifice; our lives being set apart for Him and His purposes every day. God will never accept anything from us that is second best.

Paul says we are to live our lives as living sacrifice which is our reasonable service. Reasonable is defined by many dictionaries as *logical, accepted practice, within reason and not burdensome.* That means whatever God asks us to do in our lifestyle is a living sacrifice—logical, within reason and not burdensome! We are no longer under the harsh rules of the law but under the wonderful life of Grace. We are to live our lives in a way that honours Him, a living sacrifice, daily laying our lives down for the King and His Kingdom.

What other right course of action is there for us to take? How else could we respond more appropriately to this Great God than with our lives? God in His Greatness is worthy of the complete surrender of our entire life, which is a form of worship. One of our highest callings is to be a worshipper of God in life and truth. Jesus saw the day when true worshipers would worship the Father in spirit and truth which is who the Father seeks (John 4:23). We become who we worship and when we worship God we become like Him.

> *As surely as my new heavens and earth will remain, so will you always be my people, with a name that will never disappear, says the LORD. All humanity will come to worship me from week to week and from month to month.*
> —Isaiah 66:22-23 NLT

In Heaven, after the New Earth and the New Heavens are made, all of humanity who have been justified by faith in Christ, will from week to week and month to month go and worship God from age to age. We were created to worship God forever. He alone is worthy of our worship and praise. Worship is not about what *we* get out of it but about what *God* gets out of it. We give God our best because He deserves our best.

His Ways are Higher than Our Ways

> *For my thoughts are not your thoughts, neither are your ways my ways, declares the LORD. As the heavens are higher than the earth, so are my ways higher than your ways and my thoughts than your thoughts.*
> —Isaiah 55:8-9 NIV, author's emphasis

Before we go any further, we must understand that many of the following chapters could be complex and at times not logical to our thinking. But this is exactly what faith is—choosing to accept what we can not accept. To believe what we can not yet see but know is there. That is because His thoughts are not our thoughts; His ways are not our ways (Isaiah 55:8-9). His ways are better and greater than our ways will ever be. His are built on foundations that are secure and perfect operating out of the law of love. In contrast, our ways are limited, imperfect, narrow minded and self-seeking. This radical thinking takes great faith and humility to accept. But then again, what else should we expect? It requires great faith to believe in a Great God.

It is my aim that this book will unlock the Greatness of our God to you personally. That you will discover for yourself that despite being infinite and glorious, that He is very near and desires relationship with you over anything else. This book will cover the following characteristics of God and their important counterparts which we will look at in depth:

1. **God's Mercy**: contemporary Judgement
2. **God's Goodness**: contemporary Destruction
3. **God's Grace**: contemporary Cursing's
4. **God's Love**: contemporary Wrath
5. **God's Peace**: contemporary Anxiety
6. **God's Faithfulness**: contemporary Rejection
7. **God's Abundance**: contemporary Poverty

These are by no means all of His characteristics but are a foundation of knowing an infinite God for our finite minds to comprehend. The many characteristics of God are like a priceless diamond with many sides, all different but glorious for the beholder to see. I pray that you would be enlightened and enriched by just how Great our God really is.

~ SECTION TWO ~

SECTION TWO

CHAPTER 3

The Mercy of God

Jesus Christ is the personification and complete representation of the
Mercy of God.

For I desire mercy, not sacrifice, and acknowledgment of God rather than burnt
offerings.
—Hosea 6:6 NIV

A few years ago on the country roads in southern United States, a tragic car accident
happened. A strong Christian man, loving husband, and a terrific dad, was hit
head-on by a drunk driver. The dad died on impact.

The drunk driver survived the ordeal and was facing heavy criminal charges.
Public opinion was fierce; that he should rot in prison. The punishment should
set a standard. No mercy for such an offence. The mourning family, however, were
committed Christians. They were close to one another through an invisible bond of
unconditional love. They got together and pondered out loud: What would Jesus do in
our circumstances?

One thing they knew for certain was that He would not linger in self-pity and
unforgiveness. They were convinced they had to reach out somehow to the guilty driver.
Early one morning, the son and daughter of the dad went down to the prison to visit
him. To the utter amazement of the guards, although they were deep in grief, they
hugged the man and forgave him for his actions.

The man couldn't stop his emotions from overcoming him. He crumbled to his knees and started to cry. Instead of a fist in his face, which is what he expected and knew he deserved, he received mercy. He received love instead of contempt. He received grace instead of condemnation.

Surprisingly, both the son and daughter visited him regularly and they became friends. They had truly forgiven the one who had killed their dad. Mercy proved the biggest winner at the end of the day . . . [1]

Have you ever been in a situation where you really messed up to the point where you thought you had blown it forever? Perhaps you betrayed a close friend, made a harsh comment publicly, or failed morally in private? However, what did it feel like to get another chance? When you were miraculously forgiven? The slate became clean?

Mercy is defined as '*the kind, compassionate treatment of an offender, adversary, prisoner in one's power; compassion where severity is expected, or deserved*'.[2] Among its synonyms are leniency, forgiveness, kindness and tolerance. The primary idea behind mercy is rendering kindness when a punishment is expected or even deserved. A merciful person looks beyond the present state of affairs to the potential good that may result from his compassionate handling of the matter. They are willing to forget the other's punishment or his own desire for revenge in an attempt to produce good from a bad situation.

This is the character of God every day. He imparts mercy twenty four hours a day, seven days a week. Every day we breathe His mercies are available to us when we come before Him. The tender mercies of God never fail. Every day the slate becomes clean and is a new opportunity to come humbly and boldly to the throne of grace (Hebrews 4:16).

We can do nothing to deserve or earn His Mercy. In fact we are guilty of separation and condemnation forever when we knowingly disobey His ways which are good and perfect. It is only His Mercy which is new every day that we do not receive what we should. If grace is getting what we *don't* deserve, mercy is not getting what we *do* deserve. God's condition for us to receive His mercy is simple: to confess our failings and to no longer commit them. Proverbs 28:13 says *He who covers his sins will not prosper, but whoever confesses and forsakes them will have mercy.* Our responsibility is to confess and forsake our sins so we can walk in freedom and victory.

> *Do not remember the rebellious sins of my youth. Remember me in the light of your unfailing love, for you are merciful, O LORD.*
> —Psalms 25:7 NLT

All of us can relate to Psalm 25. We have all made mistakes, either intentionally or unintentionally. We wish we could turn back time and stop them from ever happening. We have spoken words too soon without thinking to those closest to us. We have attacked and betrayed others when our pride was hurt. All of us have a long list of people impacted by our actions and behaviour. In our youth especially when we feel invincible yet lack wisdom and life experiences are our worst offences. Yet how much more does this offend God? However, God is great at forgetting our shame. In fact, He never remembers them again (Isaiah 43:25)! David had to learn this lesson well. In His unfailing love was great Mercy. Love and Mercy to God go hand in hand. They are inseparable! Be encouraged when you genuinely seek forgiveness. He remembers your mistakes no more.

Our response in receiving God's Mercy is to *give* mercy to others liberally and generously. The apostle Peter writes that we are to follow in Jesus' personal example. 1 Peter 2:21-23 says, *For even to this were you called [it is inseparable from your vocation]. For Christ also suffered for you, leaving you [His personal] example, so that you should follow in His footsteps. He was guilty of no sin, neither was deceit (guile) ever found on His lips. When He was reviled and insulted, He did not revile or offer insult in return; [when] He was abused and suffered, He made no threats [of vengeance]; but he trusted [Himself and everything] to Him Who judges fairly.* Just as He was merciful, *we also* are to show mercy in our daily judgements with others. Jesus Christ, coming down from Heaven and dying on a Cross for a sinful humanity, is the personification and complete representation of the Mercy of God.

> *Those who are well have no need of a physician, but those who are sick. But go and learn what this means: 'I desire mercy and not sacrifice.' For I did not come to call the righteous, but sinners, to repentance.*
> —Matthew 9:12-13 NKJV

Jesus shared the Mercy of God and was great at giving mercy. In saying that He desires mercy and not sacrifice, He prefers it when people practice mercy and not blindly follow ritual. He is not condemning the laws of sacrifice, but He is more pleased with acts of forgiveness and kindness than strict religious compliance.

Blessed are the Merciful

> *Blessed (happy, to be envied, and spiritually prosperous—with life—joy and satisfaction in God's favour and salvation, regardless of their outward conditions) are the merciful, for they shall obtain mercy.*
> —Matthew 5:7 AMP

These are the results of being blessed simply by being merciful to others. To be envied, spiritually prosperous, with great joy and God's favour. Only they can completely understand these invisible blessings. The word blessed is *makarios* in the Greek. Strong defines it as *happy, supremely blessed, an expression of special joy and satisfaction granted to a person who experiences salvation.*[3] It is a great feeling when you are a blessed!

We give mercy because we have received mercy from someone greater than any person could do to us. These are timing words for the world we live in today. Mercy is a rare quality these days because the world is true to its nature; it is *unmerciful.* The world values taking revenge when wronged, to repay evil for evil, and to ignore the cries of the poor and despised. Revenge is satisfying and forgiveness is admirable, but never pursued.

However, I have found being merciful has many unseen benefits. Giving mercy to others sets me free from bitterness, unforgiveness, anger and many other negative emotions that can take over my life. Choosing to let go of an offence makes you the bigger person in the relationship. Once the person sees I have forgiven them, the relationship becomes stronger with greater understanding and respect towards each other. They become a wiser person and I have become more resilient and stronger in character.

Unfortunately, people who are not merciful are constantly bound to offence. Hurting people wound hurting people. Months and years, even decades, go by and the offence is still just as fresh in their mind. But they are the ones who suffer most. They are trapped in their own prison and refuse to leave and be free. You're not always in control of your circumstances but you are always in control of how you respond to them.

The parable of the unforgiving servant is a clear example of the importance of being merciful to others. A man who owed a king many millions was forced to pay and have his family sold as slaves immediately. Upon the servants pleadings the king was moved and the debt miraculously cancelled. However, later that day a fellow servant who owed him a fraction of what he had owed the king demanded full payment. Unable to pay he had him thrown in prison. His forgetfulness cost him dearly and servants of the king advised him of what happened. The debt was again demanded and he was severely punished (see Matthew 18:21-35).

The metaphor is clear: the debt we owe God in our sins far outweighs any debt others can owe us in our lifetime. Forgiveness is at times difficult and maybe impossible. But in God's grace and strength it is possible. Even if we are ninety-eight percent not responsible for an offence, we are one hundred percent responsible for our *two* percent! To withhold mercy from others is to automatically have God withhold mercy from you in your time of need. To the measure you use will be the measure returned—always.

> *There is a destiny that makes us brothers; none goes his way alone.*
> *All that we send into the lives of others, comes back into our own.*
> —Edwin Markham, American Poet (1852-1940)

Sometimes it is harder to receive someone's mercy than to give it. Each of us can truly appreciate those who have extended mercy and forgiveness to us. They teach us a great lesson—by others spiritual maturity, in return we too should extend mercy to others. Mercy grows in us as a result of our personal experience with our Merciful God. It is an important element toward making an effective witness that we share a relationship with Him. It is God's kindness that leads to repentance (Romans 2:4). That kindness needs to be visible in the church and all the world to see. No witness is less believable than when the individual himself does contrary to what they profess to.

Mercy Triumphs over Judgement

So speak and so do as those who will be judged by the law of liberty. For judgement is without mercy to the one who has shown no mercy. Mercy triumphs over judgement.
—James 2:12-13 NKJV, author's emphasis

In all our conduct we are to act under the constant impression of the truth that we will have to give an account before God. The law of liberty is the grace made available to us through Christ. We are free to live without the slavery of sin and burdens of our old life. Our response is to think, speak and act with mercy, towards others, just as God has shown us. James says *judgement is without mercy to the one who has shown no mercy.* The law of reciprocation is always at work in our life. It follows us wherever we go. Again, the measure you use will be the measure returned. To be merciful is to receive it back from the God of Mercy. When we show compassion and kindness to those who have done us wrong, we are acting like His true children. Of course, I am not suggesting we are to become easy targets for others to take advantage of us. However, we must understand that in most cases mercy is our best option in overcoming evil with good.

Paul reiterates this in a powerful statement in Romans: *Do not repay anyone evil for evil . . . "If your enemy is hungry, feed him; if he is thirsty, give him something to drink. In doing this, you will heap burning coals on his head." Do not be overcome by evil, but overcome evil with good* (12:17; 20-21). This sounds impossible and goes against all human logic, but in actual fact it is the greatest solution. To love an enemy achieves many purposes and goals by:

1) Breaking the cycle of retaliation
2) Brings reconciliation
3) Frees us from bitterness, anger and unforgiveness
4) Overcomes evil

Just as we were once enemies to God and He made reconciliation possible, we are to do likewise with our enemies. This can be shown in many ways and contexts. To meet a physical need of providing food and water is a prime example. By loving those who have hurt us we are displaying the nature of Christ and acting as a true child of God. Jesus Himself confirmed that this is God's way: *You have heard that it was said, 'Love your neighbour and hate your enemy.' But I tell you: Love your enemies and pray for those who persecute you, that you may be sons of your Father in heaven. He causes his sun to rise on the evil and the good, and sends rain on the righteous and the unrighteous* (Matthew 5:43-45).

The effect of a person receiving love can rattle them for life. Looking back at the story from the start of the chapter, the drunk driver fell to his knees in tears when the son and daughter forgave him for killing their dad. This act of love likely led to him feeling remorse, shame, repentance and a change of heart. God desires that we show mercy towards one another. A religious life of church, prayer and reading the bible are all hollow rituals if a person does not show mercy to others in their day to day life. Even if an enemy never changes, forgiving them frees *you* from powerful negative emotions and living in bondage.

Many people would quickly lend a helping hand to another who was in physical need. But what about providing *the need of mercy* in a heated moment? Many hurting people today do not need a free meal, a holiday or a thousand dollars. They need *your mercy* extended to them with open arms. They need to be told they are forgiven and the past is forgotten. Love is patient and kind. Love keeps no record of wrongs. Love never fails at the end of the day (see 1 Corinthians 13:4-8). So, if you're like me, I need all the mercy I can get. Choose everyday to say out loud,

'*No one owes me any debt. I forgive everyone who has caused me pain or offence*'. Aim to always be in good standing with God and man. Because mercy triumphs over judgement!

The Nature of God is to be Merciful

For You, LORD, are good, and ready to forgive, and <u>abundant in mercy</u> to all those who call upon You . . . [Certainly] you are a God full of compassion, and gracious, longsuffering and <u>abundant in mercy and truth.</u>
—Psalms 86:5; 15 NLT, author's emphasis

Psalm 86 shows us an amazing quality of God's Mercy. His Mercy isn't 'just enough to get by' or 'a one off', but in fact *abundant*. Abundance refers to plentiful, rich, overflowing and lavish. We see also that His Mercy is a mixture of goodness, forgiveness, compassion, grace and longsuffering. It is based on truth, knowing all facts and details and giving a favourable verdict!

Lamentations 3:23 says, *The unfailing love of the Lord never ends! By His mercies we have been kept from complete destruction. Great is His faithfulness; His mercy is new with every day.* God's Mercy wouldn't be perfect if it wasn't forever. What is interesting is the context of when this was written. Israel had abandoned God, broken covenant and refused to repent. Judgement was complete and terrifying. They lost their promised land and were exiled to a distant country. Yet despite all this, God promised to restore His people and have them return. To a people so undeserving, God's Mercy reaches down deeper than our greatest days of shame and guilt. Even if we walk away from God in our hearts, if we confess our rebellion and turn back to Him, in His unfailing love, His Mercy will save you. Like an acrobat swinging one hundred feet in the air but a safety net is in place to catch him if he falls, so God's Mercy is our safety net. Strong and secure at all times when called upon.

For all have sinned and fall short of the glory of God, being justified freely by His grace through the redemption that is in Christ Jesus, whom God set forth as a propitiation by His blood, through faith, to demonstrate His righteousness, <u>because</u>

in His forbearance [mercy] God had passed over the sins that were previously committed.

—Romans 3:23-25 NKJV, author's emphasis and notes

Here we see one of the greatest jewels in scripture. All people have sinned and fallen short of the glory of God. Entrance into Heaven is a perfect life; a bulls-eye on a target board. Yet all have missed and fall short. All are guilty and deserve punishment. However, in spite of this, He chose another alternative for people to be saved. We are justified freely by His Grace through the redemption in Christ. The perfect life of His Son is transferred onto us through our faith. Not a head knowledge faith but a faith that is genuine and has been through the fire and proven true. Faith with testifying works, for faith without works is dead (James 2:26).

The book of Romans has many important legal terms. The devil is the accuser of the brethren, constantly throwing accusations of our sins and being unworthy to receive God's Mercy. However, heaven lives in a courtroom of Justice. Jesus is the Judge and can sympathise with our weaknesses, and the Holy Spirit is our defense attorney. Let's have a look at some important words:

1. **Justification** refers to the removal of the guilt, liability or punishment we incur through sin. When we accept Christ, God declares us righteous and we are seen to have fulfilled all that is required of us by His law; to be declared righteous before God. [4]

2. **Redemption** means to recover or buy back by paying the price; Jesus paid the price of the death penalty of sin so we can go free; the price which is paid for a prisoner of war; the ransom, or stipulated purchase-money, which being paid, the captive is set free from bondage, captivity, or evil of any kind. [5]

3. **Propitiation** refers to the appeasement of divine wrath by a sacrificial offering; the removal of God's punishment for sin through the perfect sacrifice of Jesus on the Cross. [6]

4. **Faith** is the means by which we are able to lay hold of the promises of
    God and appropriate the effects of the work of Christ in our lives.[7]

When a judge in a court of law declares the defendant not guilty, all the charges
are effectively removed from his record and no punishment is given. Legally, it is
if the person had never been accused. Likewise, the courtroom of Heaven declares
you not guilty when you belong to Christ! Don't forget who you are. Through
faith in Christ we stand acquitted with all charges against us effectively removed.

*But God is so rich in mercy, He gave us life when He raised Christ from the dead. (It
is only by God's special favour that you have been saved!) For He raised us from the
dead along with Christ, and we are seated with Him in the Heavenly realms—all
because we are one with Christ Jesus.*
—Ephesians 2:4-6 NLT

Have a look at this again. God is *so rich in mercy*. Rich is defined by most dictionaries
as expensive, valuable, generous and strong. When we were *dead* in our sins we
now have *life* with Christ. By faith we can rise above our circumstances and be
seated with God in life. It is a beautiful expression that God is rich in mercy.
Mercy is the riches or the wealth of God. People are often rich in gold and silver
and pride themselves in these possessions; but God is 'rich in mercy'. He abounds
and is so rich in it that He is willing to impart it to others; so rich that He can
make all blessed. [8]

*Surely goodness and mercy shall follow me all the days of my life, and I will dwell in
the house of the LORD forever.*
—Psalm 23:6 NLT, author's emphasis

One of the beautiful mysteries of the promises of God is that some come in pairs
and triplets. David's famous Psalm 23 has given millions around the world great
comfort and joy. When God gives *Goodness* it is always accompanied with *Mercy*.
The two can not be separated from each other for they are both Divine. They are
inseparable and close cousins, never too far apart from each other. His love and
His mercies make every day you awake a second chance. Our God is not only the

God of second chances, but of third chances and one hundred chances. His love and His mercies are new every morning; as if yesterday never happened.

We have today in front of us. It is no mistake that the world is still turning. It is no mistake that you woke up and are still breathing today. Life isn't a matter of chance or fate; life is a matter of choice. God has chosen to delay the worlds destruction by another day, and God has chosen to let you live on the earth another day. Choosing to receive His love and mercy is another matter . . .

Mercy's Contemporary: God's Judgement

I heard the sound of a vast crowd in Heaven shouting, "Hallelujah! Salvation is from our God. Glory and power belong to Him alone. <u>His Judgements are just and true</u> . . ."
—Revelation 19:2 NLT, author's emphasis

God's judgement is a difficult but necessary understanding we need to understand. It is the last action He takes when people refuse to change their ways and His warnings. A lack of judgement is not the absence of it. When judgement comes, it is delayed but fearfully destructive and completely unexpected.

Judgement is essentially a decision for or against, resulting from an investigation. It comes in different levels and different severities. Repeated sin and transgressions ultimately brings a serious punishment. This is usually administrated through people divinely orchestrated with unusual course of events, or even an act of nature. Examples of judgement can include being arrested by the police, involved in a serious car accident, broken relationships, personal injury or sickness, and loss of finances and possessions are all very possible.

The purpose of judgement ultimately is the hope people will repent of their ways and turning back to Christ. Like a punishment, its intention is for an individual to reconsider one's ways and have a change of heart. Too often, human nature is very stubborn and only a tragedy or significant event can move us. Many people are usually set in their ways and refuse to change, even for the better. Traumatic situations have the ability to change the way we believe and think.

For instance, a man who has an addiction to hoarding, collecting items of every kind, can have an event where their entire house burns down and lose everything. This has the potential to develop character changes of living a life of simplicity and generosity. A greedy woman whose character is to love money and be selfish can experience a time in her life of poverty and bankruptcy. Later, she can reflect and have a character change displaying liberality and kindness to those in need. God has given us an incredible capacity for change. A heart condition of pride, unforgiveness, judgement and bitterness are just a few reasons we need to regularly change. All are symptoms of an unsurrendered life. God is a God of many second chances. However, abusing this blessing does not continue forever.

The Day of Judgement is the last day where everyone is judged for everything we have done; both good and bad, and either rewarded or punished. *And I saw a great white throne and the one sitting on it. The earth and sky fled from his presence, but they found no place to hide. I saw the dead, both great and small, standing before God's throne. And the books were opened, including the Book of Life. And the dead were judged according to what they had done, as recorded in the books* (Revelation 20:11-12).

Hebrews 6 describes several elementary teachings of Christ, with the author pleading for believers to move on into *maturity* in their faith. One of these is 'eternal judgement'. On the Day of Judgement, all decisions handed down by the Great Judge are final and forever. Even after three trillion years, there can never be any alteration or appeal. This is why a healthy fear of God is so important. *It is a terrible thing to fall into the hands of the living God* (Hebrews 10:31).

This Divine Judgement is coming and has been ordained since the beginning of time. *For he has set a day when he will judge the world with justice by the man he has appointed. He has given proof of this to all men by raising him from the dead* (Acts 17:31). It will be done entirely fairly and justice will be perfectly delivered. God will be opposed to show any mercy to those who have not exhibited mercy and kindness to others. This is the law of reciprocation: God will judge *us* according to how we have judged *others*. For *His Judgements are just and true* (Revelation 19:12).

Sadly, I have experienced first-hand the judgement of God, and seen others either directly or indirectly. At the minimum the punishment always fits the crime. At the maximum the punishment has brought terror into my heart. I know personally when I have deliberately sinned and gone against my faith that events of bad luck and misfortune soon follow. I have experienced dreadful sicknesses, great financial cost, weeks of no peace or joy in my life, and many others.

During one season I remember always experiencing car problems. After borrowing my parents Mercedes I got terribly lost trying to pick up a friend from work late at night. I ended up completely lost and in a notoriously dangerous suburb with the car battery dead. The rest of the night was a nightmare getting myself, my friend and the car home safely, involving the whole family. This on top of starting work at 5:30am the next day! Believe me, no sin great or small is worth the trouble it brings.

Punishment speaks loudly and unconsciously reminds us of where our boundaries are. We know what acceptable behaviour is and what to avoid at all costs. Like a child being punished for disobeying commands, they must learn obedience through suffering. Psalm 119:67; 71 says, *Before I was afflicted I went astray, but now I obey your word . . . It was good for me to be afflicted, so that I might learn your decrees.* Having this understanding changes your perspective exponentially. See it for what it is worth. God may be saving you from something far worse.

Judgement Must First Begin in the House of God

> For the time has come for Judgement and *it must begin first among God's own children. And if even we Christians must be judged, what terrible fate awaits those who have never believed God's Good News?*
> —1 Peter 4:17 NLT, author's emphasis

There are varying degrees of God's Judgement: from discipline, loss of blessings, broken relationships, personal crises and misfortune, loss of finances and possessions, and ultimately death. This should not be surprising as we see this clearly throughout the Bible with story after story of God's warnings, delays, prophecies of punishment and then finally judgement.

Let's not be quick to think this is only for unbelievers but for God's people too. 1 Peter 4:17 says very clearly *For the time has come for Judgement and it must begin first among God's own children.* Before the world is judged, they will see the believers judged first so they can see for themselves what the standard of God's righteousness demands.

Jude 11 says, *They have taken the way of Cain; they have rushed for profit into Balaam's error; they have been destroyed in Korah's rebellion.* Now Cain, Korah and Balaam were all judged for murder, rebellion and love for money which led to Israel falling into idolatry. What is surprising is that at one point in time they were all serving God. It is clear that God has a high standard for His people and are to walk worthy of the calling. He expects them to be faithful and obedient to whatever He calls them to.

Other most notable examples of God's Judgement were Israel failing to enter the Promised Land. Through Abraham's faith, God chose the Hebrew nation to show Himself to the world that He is the True living God. After living in slavery for four-hundred years, they saw amazing miracles and deliverance never before seen. Their constant complaining, lack of faith and disobedience caused an entire generation to wander and die in the wilderness. However, even once in the land, their descendants soon forgot the mighty works of God and became as wicked as the nations around them. It was only until their enemies brutally subjected them that they repented, only for a generation later to run back to their useless idols (see book of Judges).

Finally, after many centuries of evil kings, leaders and prophets who abused their power and led the nation into great sin, social injustice and idolatry, they were exiled from the land. First Israel by Assyria and then Judah by Babylon. Great loss of possessions and lives were lost by continual disobedience and rebellion. Despite God's Mercy and offer of restoration and forgiveness time and time again, they refused to ever change to the point where there was no other option but judgement.

> *Do not be idolaters, as some of them were; as it is written: "The people sat down to eat and drink and got up to indulge in revelry." We should not commit sexual immorality, as some of them did—and in one day twenty-three thousand of them died. We should not test Christ, as some of them did—and were killed by snakes. And do not grumble, as some of them did—and were killed by the destroying angel. These things happened to them as examples and were written down as warnings for us, on whom the culmination of the ages has come.*
> —1 Corinthians 10:7-11 NIV, author's emphasis

Their actions serve as a strong warning and prime examples to us today. Twenty-three thousand people is a small nation—that's a bad day! Just as Israel was set free but went back into slavery, so can the believer. Our response to God's Judgement should be to have a godly fear, faithfulness and obedience. A good father shows his love by discipline and correction when required. Hebrews says, *Endure hardship as discipline; God is treating you as sons. For what son is not disciplined by his father? If you are not disciplined (and everyone undergoes discipline), then you are illegitimate children and not true sons. Moreover, we have all had human fathers who disciplined us and we respected them for it. How much more should we submit to the Father of our spirits and live! Our fathers disciplined us for a little while as they thought best; but God disciplines us for our good, that we may share in his holiness* (12:7-10, author's emphasis). Discipline is a sign of God's Love for us as legitimate children. Absence of discipline means absence of relationship. This is the nature of God to His true children.

> *Let the wicked forsake his way, and the unrighteous man his thoughts; let him return to the LORD, and He will have mercy on him; and to our God, for He will abundantly pardon.*
> —Isaiah 55:7 NKJV

To the skeptic it would be easy for one to assume God as angry and blood thirsty when He brings judgement just looking at the Old Testament. But this is certainly not the case. Scripture clearly shows again and again the heart of God who is *ready* to forgive and *abundant* in mercy. If people simply draw near to Him, humble themselves, pray, seek His face, and turn from their wicked ways, then God promises to hear from Heaven, forgive their sins and heal their land (2 Chronicles 7:14). Let's now look at a crystal clear example from scripture where we see Mercy mixed with Judgement.

Example: Jonah—God's Unwilling Prophet

> *Now the word of the LORD came to Jonah the son of Amittai, saying,*
> *"Arise, go to Nineveh, that great city, and cry out against it;*
> *for their wickedness has come up before Me."*
> —Jonah 1:1-2 NKJV

A great example of God's Mercy is found in the small book of Jonah. God calls Jonah to tell the evil people of Ninevah to repent of their ways or destruction will come in forty days. Ninevah were a violent and war like nation. History tells us that their war tactics were so brutal and inhumane as an attempt to have their enemies surrender on their arrival. They were people who showed no mercy towards others. As a result, God's judgement would repay their lack of mercy. However, in order for God to be true to His nature in Judgement, there must always be Mercy with Judgement (forty days to repent). God's Judgement is always delayed, but always certain and always terrifying.

> *But <u>Jonah ran away from the Lord</u> and headed for Tarshish.*
> *He went down to Joppa, where he found a ship bound for that port.*
> *<u>After paying the fare,</u> he went aboard and sailed for*
> *Tarshish to flee from the Lord.*
> —Jonah 1:3 NIV, author's emphasis

In a sense, Jonah was right to run away from God's request. They were not God's people or shared a special covenant relationship with Him. They were outsiders and deserved God's Judgement. They were unmerciful to others so they deserved to be shown no mercy. They deserved destruction and God's wrath. Yet God's mercy is greater than people's sin. This was their response:

> *The people of Nineveh <u>believed God's message</u>, and from the greatest to the least, they declared a fast and put on burlap (the culture of the day as a public sign of repentance) to show their sorrow. When the king of Nineveh heard what Jonah was saying, he stepped down from his throne and took off his royal robes. He dressed himself in burlap and sat on a heap of ashes. Then the king and his nobles sent this decree throughout the city: "No one, not even the animals from your herds and flocks, may eat or drink anything at all. People and animals alike must wear garments of mourning, and everyone must pray earnestly to God. <u>They must turn from their evil ways and stop all their violence</u>. Who can tell? Perhaps even yet God will change his mind and old back his fierce anger from destroying us." When God saw what they had done and how they had put a stop to their evil ways, he changed his mind and did not carry out the destruction he had threatened.*
> —Jonah 3:5-10 NLT, author's emphasis

The people responded to Jonah's message from God and repented, from the greatest to the least. Jonah knew the ways of God. That He was abundant in mercy and forgiveness. I have a feeling Jonah knew this all along that God would pardon Ninevah. For he later says, *For I know that You are a gracious and merciful God, slow to anger and abundant in loving-kindness, One who relents from doing harm* (Jonah 4:2). Are you catching on to this? God's nature is that He is *always* gracious and merciful whenever possible. It is not always forever when one refuses to change, but it is always long enough in duration for the individual to come to their senses and see the error in their ways.

God is unwilling and reluctant to cause harm to any person made in His image. The Amplified version reads . . . *for I knew that You are a gracious God and merciful, slow to anger and of great kindness, and [when sinners turn to You and meet Your conditions] You revoke the [sentence of] evil against them* (Jonah 4:2). Amazing. Surely God's Mercy is new every morning. His abundant mercy is a fragrance that is strong. His Mercy transforms all those who accept it.

Sadly, history however tells us that the next generation of the people of Nineveh picked up their parents wicked ways. The world power of Assyria was soon overthrown by the nation of Babylon and Judgement came as promised (see book of Nahum). No characteristic of God's disqualifies another. In His Holiness He brings Justice. In His Mercy He brings Love. And in His Righteousness He brings Judgement.

Important Lessons

Let's not miss several key lessons in this short story in Jonah's life. When God specifically spoke to him with instructions to go to Nineveh, he deliberately disobeyed and went in the complete opposite direction. I have a feeling God knew in advance that Jonah would run away from the call of God but would eventually be His 'unwilling prophet'. Jonah was self-righteous and God probably chose him to be His messenger of warning to teach *him* a few things in the process.

A key point in Jonah's rebellion was that 'he paid the fare' to Tarshish but never reached his destination. It always costs the believer personally to backslide—either financially, physically or relationally. It is one thing for an unbeliever to ignore God knocking at the door of their heart, but another for a believer to willfully run away and be disobedient to their calling. As God's children we are all called to be ambassadors for Christ, pleading with others to be reconciled to God on every occasion (2 Corinthians 5:20).

Jonah travelled by boat to Tarnish, a powerful storm arose and all on board almost perished. The sailor's casted lots (a type of superstitious lottery system that identified people) to see who was responsible for 'making the gods angry'. Even these pagan sailors feared God more than Jonah. Knowing he was completely at fault, Jonah was suicidal and told the men to throw him overboard, knowing that the storm would stop.

When a man prefers to die rather than change, it takes an incredibly merciful God to intervene and be patient long enough until he does God's work. We must understand that judgement *first* came to the godly Jonah, not the wicked

Nineveh. This is because judgement must first begin among God's own people (1 Peter 4:17). Jonah now with no other way out travels to Ninevah to pronounce judgement on his enemies. However, they believe his message and the entire nation repents of their evil ways. God's judgement ceases and the nation is spared.

It is ironic that Jonah's response is anger and self-righteousness at God's Mercy. He was angry that God had shown mercy instead of showing judgement. Theologians suggest that the reason he ran away was because of his pride in being a prophet—that what he said would always come true. Now that God's Mercy overruled His judgement by the law of repentance, Jonah replied '*Just kill me now, Lord! I'd rather be dead than alive because nothing I predicted is going to happen*' (Jonah 4:3). Amazing! During Jonah's pity potty moment, he was now suicidal again because what he said would now not come to pass. May we never judge others to this extreme level and take up the office by our own election 'accuser of the wicked'. May we instead show mercy to others, just as God is merciful towards us.

Final Thoughts

God's Mercy is always available to those who seek it diligently. He doesn't ration His Mercy, as though it were in short supply. His Mercy is unlimited as long as we continue to genuinely seek it, confess our failures and change our ways. It is expected that we as the righteous show mercy and give mercy when required. Only the wicked and those who have no understanding of the Mercy shown to them give no mercy.

Don't ever think that you've crossed the line and can't be forgiven anymore, or you've reached a point where God can't use you anymore. As long as you have breath in your lungs, you are forgivable and redeemable. Our physical death is where God's Mercy and Judgement become permanent, depending on how we have lived. Sometimes we can think God is far too lenient with others and way too hard on us. He alone is the judge. He knows best and sees all of time. Remember, our role is to trust Him and have faith—not help Him try to do His job better! So, who can you show mercy to today?

CHAPTER 4

The Goodness of God

Faith is the complete dependence on the Goodness of God. It is
not just a theological fact but something that can be personally
experienced.

Oh give thanks to the LORD, for He is good: for His mercy endures forever . . .
Oh that men would praise the Lord for His goodness, and His wonderful works
to the children of men. For He satisfies the hungry soul with goodness.
—Psalms 107:1; 8-9 NKJV

*I can still remember that late summer night when I was eleven. My grandmother's
scream woke me from my sleep. My brother grabbed me out of bed and yelled there was
a fire out of control in the house. We only had seconds to live. In a daze and confusion
we ran through the smoke filled rooms. Mum saw our little dog at the last instant,
picking him up as we ran out the front door.*

*Finally, all of us were standing on the street in the pitch dark wearing only the night
clothes we were sleeping in. We watched helpless as grandma's fifty year old house
burned to the ground in a matter of minutes along with everything we owned. I can
still see my mum, dad, brothers, grandma, and I standing there crying and wondering
what we were going to do after losing everything we had.*

*However, every essential thing that we needed had come out that door with us. Our
hearts, minds, bodies, and souls were all unhurt and that was all we needed to live in
love and joy again. We were still a family. We were still together. We could still hold
each other, laugh, and share our love and happiness at being alive. Soon thanks to our*

community and extended family we had replaced what material things we had lost and moved into another home. Life eventually went back to normal.

While pondering this event years later, I learnt a powerful lesson. It was only then that I realised that God had, in fact, spared us from losing the one true treasure each of us had: our lives. God's Goodness was all that mattered and was all we needed. A lesson I'll never forget . . . [1]

The Goodness of God is declared right from the beginning in the account of Creation. Repeatedly, God pronounces everything He created as 'good'. Ultimately, all that originates from God can not be anything but good and wonderful: *And God saw everything that He had made, and, behold, it was very good* (Genesis 1:31).

Goodness is defined as *kindness, dispensing of good and wonderful gifts, compassion, helpfulness, gifts that are pleasant, lovely and enjoyable; to someone's benefit, advantage or profit.* [2] Goodness comes naturally to God. He is always good—He does not have to work at it. It is made visible in what He does for His people. His Goodness keeps us from harm, provides our needs, and leads us on paths of peace and rest. His Goodness is His abundant overflow of unmerited gifts to all people, good and bad, especially His offer of salvation by means of His Son which all people can be saved.

Psalm 107 tells us we are to give Him thanks *because* He is Good. There is much to be thankful for: the gift of life, loving family and friends, meaning and purpose in work and study, salvation, the Holy Spirit and many others. We are to give thanks to the LORD for He is Good. Scripture does not hold back declaring God being given all praise and thanks, simply for the fact that He is Good. Our thanks must be directed at God; not ecosystems, objects, people or processes—God! Everything He created was for our personal enjoyment, so we could *fully* experience His Goodness every day.

God didn't create us as robots without the ability to feel love, joy, pain and sadness. He created us as highly emotional, physical, intellectual beings. We can learn, reason and analyse complex formulas and challenges. He created us with senses that can touch objects, taste delicious foods, smell fragrances, hear fine music and see stunning sunsets. We can find incredible meaning and purpose in achievements, relationships and solving problems. From this He created a world where we can experience the joy of tasting food, the pleasure of working a long hard day, delight in relaxing and having meaningful hobbies and interests. He created a world where we could fully enjoy good things every day. And He created us with an unlimited imagination and to dream of the impossible.

> *Man alone has the power to transform his thoughts into physical reality.*
> *Man, alone, can dream and make his dreams come true.*
> —Napoleon Hill, American author (1883-1970)

The Goodness of God is a foundational truth that shapes our perspective toward God and His dealings with us. When a foundation is strong it lasts a lifetime. Fierce storms and winds may come and go but the building is still standing every time. Faith in the character of God is the greatest place to put our trust. Faith in the complete dependence on the Goodness of God is to place your life on a firm foundation that can not be shaken. Psalms 62:1-2 says, *My soul finds rest in God alone; my salvation comes from him. He alone is my rock and my salvation; he is my fortress, I will never be shaken.* Scripture literally abounds everywhere on God's Goodness. Some of the many passages include His Goodness being:

1) **Great**—Nehemiah 9:35
2) **Rich**—Psalms 104:24
3) **Abundant**—Exodus 34:6
4) **Universal**—Psalms 145:9
5) **Given to those who fear Him**—Psalm 31:19
6) **For His people**—Psalm 119:68
7) **For the forgiveness of sin**—Psalm 86:5

If our eyes are open, we will see His Goodness follow us, pursue and run us over! Sometimes it is well hidden and then becomes a surprise in an unexpectant moment, to maximise our delight and joy. The Goodness of God is the overall summation of His everything that He is. Apart from God, we can not even begin to understand what true Goodness is, for it can not be understood apart from Him, the author of Goodness.

Psalm 145:7; 9 says, *They will celebrate your <u>abundant goodness,</u> and joyfully sing of your righteousness . . . The Lord is <u>good to all;</u> He has compassion on all He has made* (author's emphasis). God's Goodness is revealed in His works of creation. Our response is to celebrate and sing joyfully. The reason for God's Goodness is His compassion to all He has made. Compassion is often defined as kindness, concern, care and gentleness. People who believe God is distant and angry do not realise how completely wrong they are. Their thinking is distorted and has no foundation. He is our God and we are His people. For the Lord is good to all, He has compassion on all He has made.

> *He said to them, "Go into all the world and preach the <u>good news</u> to all creation . . ."*
> —Mark 16:15 NIV, author's emphasis

It is no mistake that the gospel is Good News! The Cross is a plus sign, not a negative. Faith is the complete dependence on the Goodness of God. It is not just a theological fact but it is something that can be personally experienced. It is your personal assurance that God's character is entirely trustworthy; regardless of our circumstances, good or bad.

Nothing can ever satisfy in life using a substitute for God. I have found many times in moments of *fear*, there is no place on earth I can go where I can gain permanent peace apart from God's presence. In times of *pain* and *sorrow*, there is no where I can go to experience healing and comfort apart from God. And in *loneliness* and craving for love and affirmation, there is no where the hole in my heart can be filled apart from God. This is the Goodness of God. Nothing this world has to offer can satisfy a person forever apart from Him.

The longer I live the more deeply involved I see God's powerfully involved in my life. He is personally interested in my dreams, my desires, my success and my ultimate well-being in life. He is completely committed to my ultimate best interests and highest success. He has healed me from a broken past, kept me safe in dangerous situations and brought reconciliation to my family. He has amazing and good plans for my life and desires nothing less than to give me to have a life more abundantly. This is the Greatness of our God!

The Nature of God is to Show Goodness

And as He was setting out on His journey, a man ran up and knelt before Him and asked Him, <u>Good [You are essentially and perfectly morally good] Teacher</u>, what must I do to inherit eternal life [to partake of eternal salvation in the Messiah's kingdom]? And Jesus said to him, Why do you call Me [essentially and perfectly morally] good? There is no one [essentially and perfectly morally] good—except God alone.
—Mark 10:17-18 AMP, author's emphasis

God's greatest demonstration of His Goodness was sending His only Son to die on a Cross in our place of punishment. The Bible tells us mankind follows only the works of darkness, deserving of God's eternal wrath. *And you were dead in the trespasses and sins in which you once walked, following the course of this world, following the prince of the power of the air, the spirit that is now at work in the sons of disobedience—among whom we all once lived in the passions of our flesh, carrying out the desires of the body and the mind, and were by nature children of wrath, like the rest of mankind* (Ephesians 2:1-3). But God in His Goodness has made possible a way by which we may escape Judgement, and can spend eternity in His presence. Out of this Goodness He gives each man the choice to either accept or reject His Son. After all, He is too good to force a decision on anyone's free will. To deny His Son is to therefore deny His Greatest act of Goodness mankind will ever know.

Jesus made a startling statement which is easily passed over by many. When a man in public one day ran up to Him and said 'Good Teacher', he was effectively saying whether he realised it or not, Jesus was God. In the Jewish culture which was highly religious, they only referred to God as Good, for they understood that they themselves, no matter how perfect of righteous they could be, could never meet up to the standard of God's Goodness. By the man calling Jesus 'Good Teacher' he was essentially saying Jesus was God. This was well before Jesus revealed His true deity publically. Either deliberately or unknowingly the man was saying Jesus was God. In response, Jesus confirmed that God alone is Good, and being His Son, He too was Good, for He was God in the flesh.

> *Oh, taste and see that the LORD is good;*
> *blessed is the man who trusts in Him!*
> —Psalm 34:8 NLT

Here we see an amazing invitation. Tangibly we can experience for ourselves through our senses the Goodness of God. By simply trusting in Him you are already blessed! Our Spirit man has a duplicate set of feelings and functions as our physical man. They are divinely combined. Just as we can taste the amazing explosion of flavours from biting into a fresh watermelon on a hot summer's day, our Spirit can taste the Goodness of God in His presence. Just as we can see a table surrounded by loving family and friends, we can see the Goodness of God in our lives that we are blessed with amazing relationships.

People can be good, morally and ethically. But using God's standard of good no one comes close. *God looks down from heaven upon the children of men, to see if there are any who understand, who seek God. Every one of them has turned aside; they have together become corrupt; there is none who does good, no, not one* (Psalms 53:3). Yet despite this truth, God is good to all; He has compassion on all He has made. If the tables were turned and you were God, would you be so willing to show Goodness to your creation who had rebelled against you? Yet God in His Greatness is the same yesterday, today and forever. *He causes his sun to rise on the evil and the good, and sends rain on the righteous and the unrighteous* (Matthew 5:45).

Common Goodness versus Great Goodness

> *How great is Your Goodness! You have stored it up for those who fear you.*
> *You do good things for those who trust you. You do this for all to see.*
> —Psalm 31:19 NLT

It can be seen that there are different levels of experiencing God's Goodness. There is a *common goodness* and a *great goodness*. *Common goodness* is universally known to most people. It is to experience the simple pleasures of life, to enjoy relationships, and to work productively. However, it is limited. Life is always challenging and frustrating, inner peace is distant, and there is constant friction in relationships. Instead of seeing everything they do have they concentrate on their lack and never have enough.

Then there is *special goodness* reserved for those who fear God and obey His ways. This is to live in favour, to be blessed when you walk in and blessed when you walk out. It is to live life free from sicknesses, and relationships are always blessed. Life works out and no one knows why! Psalm 84:11 says, *For the LORD God is a sun and shield; The LORD gives grace and glory; <u>No good thing does He withhold from those who walk uprightly</u>* (author's emphasis).

Obedience to His ways always brings an unlimited open heaven over your life. It is simply not possible for God to withhold good and wonderful things to those who walk uprightly. The smile of God shines constantly over their paths and a shield of protection covers them in the face of danger. God does good things for those who trust Him. It is a strong place to be when your trust is completely surrendered to His leading. God is Good to all men in His common goodness, showering blessings on the wicked and the righteous alike. But more importantly, He is particularly Good to those who believe and obey Him completely.

> *You know with all your heart and soul that <u>not one of all the good promises the Lord your God gave you has failed</u>. Every promise has been fulfilled; not one has failed.*
> —Joshua 23:14 NIV, author's emphasis

God will be in debt to no man. He delivers on all of His promises. God is not a liar—whatever He says will come to pass. With that in mind every promise has a *premise*. The blessings, anointing and favour of God all come with a price tag. Obedience to His ways is the key to this treasure. Our response to His Goodness is nothing less than gratitude and thankfulness. It should be expectant and delighted in by His people regularly. *Be joyful always; pray continually; give thanks in all circumstances, for this is God's will for you in Christ Jesus* (1 Thessalonians 5:16-18). Unthankfulness was the first state of mind that led to Adam and Eve being deceived and taking from the forbidden fruit. When we are unthankful, we are in a place of self-centeredness. We believe life is all about us and whatever pleases self is priority. But when we are thankful, we will see with eyes beyond our life and look upon everything good that God has done for us.

The Goodness of God Leads to Repentance

> *Or do you despise the riches of His goodness, forbearance, and longsuffering,*
> *not knowing that the goodness of God leads you to repentance?*
> —Romans 2:4 NKJV

When Billy Graham was driving through a small southern town in the States, he was stopped by a policeman and charged with speeding. Graham admitted his guilt and was told by the officer he would have to go to court. On the day the judge asked, "*Guilty, or not guilty?*" When Graham pleaded guilty, the judge replied, "*That'll be ten dollars—a dollar for every mile you went over the limit.*"

Suddenly the judge recognised the famous minister. "*You have violated the law,*" he said. "*The fine must be paid—but I am going to pay it for you.*" He took a ten dollar bill from his own wallet, attached it to the ticket, and then took Graham out and bought him a steak dinner! "*That,*" said Billy Graham, "*is how God treats repentant sinners!*" [4]

It is likely that the Goodness of God has led you and me to accept Jesus as our Lord and Saviour. The Bible shows us it is the Goodness of God which leads one to repentance. People do not respond to the fear of hell, judgement and condemnation. People respond to God by His Goodness. Fear of punishment wears off after a while. Yet goodness can last a lifetime. Most people turn to God, not because of fear of punishment, but because they find out that He is the only solution to their problems.

Years ago before I came to Christ, while overseas I watched the movie *The Exorcist* and was visibly shaken afterwards. I remember thinking to myself, 'I will never ever sin again!' But surely after a few days, the memories of the scenes disappeared and I went on living my life again. I experienced for the first time the fear of God, but didn't have the ability to repent from my lifestyle. A year later when my life fell apart at the end of a serious long term relationship, I experienced the unconditional love of God and His offer of forgiveness. I was never the same again.

I read a story recently of a professor who asked his class to pray for his wife who was going to see the doctor because of some symptoms which might indicate cancer. He reported the tests were negative and his wife's cancer had subsided. He later told the class that had the doctor's report been that his wife did have cancer, God is still good. He knew what we also must know if we are to think biblically about the Goodness of God—He is always good, whether He sends prosperity or pain, sickness or health.

Some people seem to think that once they are saved that God for some reason withdraws His Goodness! They think He puts us through tragedy, sickness, pain, poverty, temptations and a multitude of trials to teach us a lesson. Such thinking is only lies from the enemy. Once we have come into the Kingdom of God He does not give us less of His Goodness. He bestows upon us more and more, though in our busyness we may not see them. Jesus never promised a life free from problems. In fact He said, *Here on earth you will have many trials and sorrows. But take heart, because I have overcome the world* (John 16:33). Tests and trials strengthen us so we can be strong in faith. Then when we are mature we can correctly handle all the good things God desires to give to us.

Goodness's Contemporary: Destruction

The Lord Himself will send against you curses, confusion and disillusionment in everything you do, <u>until at last you are completely destroyed</u> for doing evil and forsaking me . . . Because you have not served the Lord your God with joy and enthusiasm for the abundant benefits you have received, you will serve your enemies . . . <u>They will oppress you harshly until you are destroyed.</u>
—Deuteronomy 28:20; 47-48 NLT, author's emphasis

The doctrine of destruction is a difficult but essential truth we must know. The person who persistently refuses to change their ways and repent from sin after seeing the Goodness of God will finally be punished. God is patient for our sake so that few will perish. 2 Peter 3:9 says, *The Lord is not slow in keeping His promise, as some understand slowness. He is patient with you, not wanting anyone to perish, but everyone to come to repentance.* But be sure time will eventually run out. Scripture is clear that the Goodness of God *expects* results of repentance; a change of heart, mind and lifestyle. His Goodness is not to be abused or taken advantage of. If we reject His Goodness, refuse to turn from our ways, and reject the gospel, then we will eventually bring upon ourselves His destruction.

The goodness of God is seen in that when man transgressed the law of His Creator a dispensation of unmixed wrath did not at once commence . . . Would God be 'good' if He punished not those who ill-use His blessings, abuse His benevolence, and trample His mercies beneath their feet? It will be no reflection upon God's Goodness, but rather the brightest exemplification of it, when He shall rid the earth of those who have broken His laws, defied His authority, mocked His messengers, scorned His Son, and persecuted those for whom He died.
—Arthur Walkington Pink, evangelist and author (1886-1952)[3]

In total contrast to God's Goodness, hell is a place totally void of all that is good. It is a place of utter evil, death, darkness and condemnation. Hell is where people are permanently cut off from all things on earth that we enjoy and take for granted. There are no relationships but isolation. No meaningful work or activities but pain and horror. There is no peace or rest but constant torture.[5] Many scriptures speak in great detail of the reality of hell:

Terrors startle him on every side and dog his every step. Calamity is hungry for him; disaster is ready for him when he falls. It eats away parts of his skin; death's firstborn devours his limbs. He is torn from the security of his tent and marched off to the king of terrors. Fire resides in his tent; burning sulfur is scattered over his dwelling. His roots dry up below and his branches wither above. The memory of him perishes from the earth; he has no name in the land. He is driven from light into darkness and is banished from the world. He has no offspring or descendants among his people, no survivor where once he lived. Men of the west are appalled at his fate; men of the east are seized with horror. Surely such is the dwelling of an evil man; such is the place of one who knows not God."
—Job 18:11-21 NIV

God's Goodness is a character trait which applies to every other one of His attributes. Because He is perfect, all His ways are perfect. This means that God's wrath is good. God's holiness is good. God's judgement is good. Just as God's Goodness is certain to those who live for Him, it is just as certain those who reject His Goodness will come to ruin. They have tested the Lord long enough and there will be no escape of punishment. Their strength will fail in their time of need, and they will lose everything they have worked for. By their will, they will finally be cut off from the Goodness of their God, forever.

Example—A Psalm of Asaph

Surely God is good to Israel, to those who are pure in heart . . .
—Psalm 73:1 NIV

The central theme of Psalm 73 is the Goodness of God. The first and the last verses contain the word 'good' but both give radically different perspectives. The author, Asaph, describes a period in his life when he had serious spiritual struggles. His initial understanding was that because God is Good to His people, he will live a pain free life. Meanwhile, outsiders will have nothing to look forward to but many difficulties, misery and pain. Now there is an element of truth in this, as we can see from the blessings and cursings of Deuteronomy 28. But this is simply not always the case as he soon found out:

> *But as for me, my feet came close to stumbling; My steps had almost slipped.*
> *For I was envious of the arrogant, when I saw the prosperity of the wicked.*
> —Psalms 73:2-3 NIV

Asaph admits that he strayed far off course. He was so far from the truth that he came close to destruction as he envied the wicked. He seems to be confessing almost giving up the faith and forsaking the way of righteousness, supposing it was of no real benefit. His thoughts were probably, *If God is Good why am I depressed and the wicked prospering? Why am I angry and going through adversity? And why are my relationships on the rocks and I'm struggling right now?*

This is a common misperception for most believers today. They think, *if God is not blessing me then He must be ignoring me and I'm not worth His Goodness. I've done something wrong and He doesn't love me anymore.* Like Asaph, their problem is largely due to their distorted perspective. First of all, he was envious of the wicked. To envy is to forget all the blessings God has given you and focus on others and compare what you currently do not have. Asaph wished he could be in their shoes. He did not hate their sin; he envied their success. Second, he was self-righteous. He looked upon himself as being better than he was. He seems to have supposed he deserved better from God and concluded his righteous living had been in vain.

Asaph continues to make sweeping generalisations in the first half of the psalm, implying that all the wicked prosper and the righteous, which surely included him, suffer. He wrongly supposes the wicked are always happy and thinks none of the wicked experience the difficulties of life. Even in their death, they are somehow spared from discomfort. He likewise thinks those who prosper are all arrogant, blaspheming God, daring Him to know or care about what the wicked are doing.[6]

If I had really spoken this way to others, I would have been a traitor to your people.
So I tried to understand why the wicked prosper. But what a difficult task it is!
Then I went into your sanctuary, O God, and I finally understood the destiny of the
wicked.

—Psalms 73:15-17 NLT

The turning point for Asaph is verse fifteen. Up to this point, he viewed life from a distorted religious view. To him, the Goodness of God meant him being 'happy, healthy and wealthy'. But Asaph admits he was wrong. When he came into the sanctuary of God, he was able to perceive their end. Now he viewed the prosperity of the wicked in the light of eternity rather than here and now which soon disappears. Those who seemed to be doing so well in their wickedness Asaph now saw in great peril. Their feet were on a slippery place. In but a short time, they would face the Judgement of God. Their payday for sin might not come immediately, but it would surely come.

Surely you place them on slippery ground; you cast them down to ruin. How suddenly
are they destroyed, completely swept away by terrors! As a dream when one awakes, so
when you arise, O Lord, you will despise them as fantasies . . . Yet I am always with
you; you hold me by my right hand. You guide me with your counsel, and afterward
you will take me into glory. Whom have I in heaven but you? And earth has nothing
I desire besides you. My flesh and my heart may fail, but God is the strength of my
heart and my portion forever.

—Psalms 73:18-20; 23-26 NIV

How foolish Asaph had been to think the wicked would get away with their sin, and there would be no day of reckoning. How foolish to conclude God was punishing him for avoiding the sinful ways of the wicked. Asaph now sees that the prosperity of the wicked has hardened their hearts. They have become proud, arrogant, and independent towards God.[7] *Salvation is far from the wicked, for they do not seek out your decrees* (Psalm 119:155).

He now sees his relationship with God in its true light. Life is really a dream and eternity is waking up. In his short term pain, there was long term gain. Eternity holds for him the bright hope of God's glorious presence. But in addition to this future blessing, Asaph has the pleasure of God's presence in this life. Now he sees his affliction as a source of great blessing. His suffering drew him closer to God; but the prosperity of the wicked drew them away. In the final verses, he explains why he was wrong, ending with an entirely different definition of 'good':

> *Those who desert him will perish, for you destroy those who abandon you. But as for me, how good it is to be near God! I have made the Sovereign LORD my shelter, and I will tell everyone about the wonderful things you do.*
> —Psalm 73:27-28 NLT

Asaph understood the Goodness of God in a different light. In verse one, 'good' meant the absence of pain, difficulty, trouble, sorrow, ill health, or poverty. In verse twenty-eight, 'good' means to be near to God and enjoy intimate fellowship. We may say then that whatever interferes with our fellowship with Him is actually evil. And whatever draws us into a deeper fellowship with God is actually good. When God brings suffering and adversity into our lives, our confidence in His Goodness should not be undermined. Instead, we should be reassured and at peace of His Goodness to us.

As Asaph indicates, along with countless others in the world, suffering is often the means by which we come to know God more intimately. You may ask, "*Why do people who ignore God, hate Him and still prosper while those who live for Him and love Him suffer?*" Well, not in the long run. First things first, why are you comparing? If you hadn't of looked and compared what they have to you, then you wouldn't be thinking this. Secondly, see the bigger picture. You are saved and your eternal destiny secured. You are loved by the Father. Heaven awaits you! Have perspective that there is a purpose in every season. What is He teaching you and what areas in your life need to change? His aim is for you to measure up to the full stature of Christ (Ephesians 4:13). This is the high call of God.

Asaph's trials were indeed a gift from God for his good. His struggles led him into a deeper intimacy with God and were now worth all the temporary distress to his soul. His faith had been tested and proven genuine. Trusting God and living a holy life prove we are His people. It is not the reason we get blessed but a byproduct in due time. *Let us not become weary in doing good, for at the proper time we will reap a harvest if we do not give up* (Galatians 6:9).

God's Goodness is Nearness in the Face of Adversity

I want to know Christ and experience the mighty power that raised him from the dead. I want to suffer with him, sharing in his death, so that one way or another I will experience the resurrection from the dead!
—Philippians 3:10-11 NLT

We are never more nearer to God and more closer to Him than in the midst of adversity. It is often a time when people either run far from God and blame Him for their circumstances. Or it is a time when people run to Him for healing, answers and deliverance. Adversities and hardship can come in many ways and contexts. Ultimately, it is best described as a place of brokenness; when you have come to the end of yourself. This is where who you really are and everything in your heart comes out. It is this time that we must draw near to God and seek His face. Psalm 34:17-19 says, *The righteous cry out, and the LORD hears them; he delivers them from all their troubles.* <u>*The LORD is close to the brokenhearted and saves those who are crushed in spirit.*</u> *A righteous man may have many troubles, but the LORD delivers him from them all* (authors' emphasis).

Personally, I have experienced moments of great sorrow and brokenness many times. Growing up in a divorced family, I always struggled academically, making friends and battled low self-confidence. As a child, all I knew were fear, emotional trauma and rejection. I have been well acquainted with chronic depression, and on two occasions I seriously considered suicide. After one very difficult and testing year, I came to the end of myself and hit rock bottom. My relationships with peers were strained, my family hit a new level of intense conflict, and a separate incident led me to a faith crash. For four weeks I had an emotional breakdown. All I could do was cry and do basic tasks. Dark thoughts clouded my mind and judgement. I lost all vision and purpose in life. It felt like I had walked into a dark forest and couldn't find my way out. Finally I cried out to God for comfort and answers. At a time of unbearable grief I lifted my hands to God in surrender and worship, giving everything to Him. Through a gradual process, I was healed and set free. I had been through the fire and come forth as gold (Job 23:10).

Words can not describe the joy and happiness that came upon me. I was restored and made new. Every morning I would wake up at dawn and watch the sunrise to pray and seek God. (To those who know me, I am not a morning person!) I saw heaven and touched my glory. Psalms 90:14-15 says, *Satisfy us in the morning with your unfailing love, that we may sing for joy and be glad all our days. Make us glad for as many days as you have afflicted us, for as many years as we have seen trouble.* The most powerful worship in the world is when your hands are lifted high and your heart is completely broken. In the midst of chaos and despair, your soul is abandoned to the Father's heart. Your faith is anchored to the Saviour. God's greatest servants are people of brokenness who have been made whole. His greatest churches will be built on the brokenness of His people, being made new into His image.

The apostle Paul confirmed this who went through unspeakable trials and adversity planting churches all over Asia Minor. *I want to know Christ and experience the mighty power that raised him from the dead. I want to suffer with him, sharing in his death, so that one way or another I will experience the resurrection from the dead!* (Philippians 3:10). Paul's heart was to be fully acquainted with God's nature and His salvation; one of the highest objects of desire we can ever know. And in the midst of his sufferings, this was where he drew the closest. God's Goodness, is nearness to Him, even in a time of adversity.

Paul desired to participate in the same kind of sufferings that Christ endured, so as to be identified with Him. He wished to be just like his Saviour. He felt that it was an honour to live as He did; to possess the Spirit that He did, and to suffer in the same manner if necessary. All that Christ did was glorious in his view, and he wished in all things to resemble Him. He did not desire merely to share His honours and triumphs in heaven, but regarding His whole work as wonderful, he wished to be fully conformed and as far as possible to be just like Christ.[8]

Many are willing to reign with Christ, but they would not be willing to suffer with Him. Many would be willing to wear a crown of glory like Him, but not the crown of thorns. And many would be willing to put on the robes of splendour which will be worn in heaven, but not the scarlet robe of contempt and mockery. They would desire to share the glories and triumphs of redemption, but not its poverty and persecution. This was not the feeling of Paul. He wished in all things to be just like Christ, and counted it an honour to be permitted to suffer as He did
—Anonymous

Peter shared this same feeling: *But rejoice, since you are partakers of Christ's sufferings; that, when his glory shall be revealed, you may be glad also with exceeding joy* (1 Peter 4:13). It is an honour to suffer as Christ suffered. The true Christian will esteem it a privilege to be made just like Him; not only in glory, but in trials and adversities as well. Ultimately, the trials we go through are specifically orchestrated by God according to the character qualities we need to still develop, for the future plans God has in store for us.

Does it mean he no longer loves us if we have trouble or calamity, or are persecuted, or hungry, or destitute, or in danger, or threatened with death? . . . No, despite all these things, overwhelming victory is ours through Christ, who loved us.
—Romans 8:35; 37 NLT

Now I am not at all saying that God takes delight in our adversities and doesn't want us to be happy and healthy. What is true is that He loves us deeply, but loves us too much to stay the same. God is more concerned about our faith and character growing more than our comfort and convenience. Adversity is a place where faith and character grow the fastest. He wants us to be happy, but then He needs us to grow up too. To put away our childish ways and become mature in Christ.

Final Thoughts

The Goodness of God is a life-transforming revelation. We must believe with all certainty and have no doubt that our God is a Good God in every way. There is nothing about Him that is simply not good. As a leader, keep reminding your people of the Goodness of God. I believe it is something people will never get tired of hearing.

There is nothing God purposes for His children that is not good. This means He withholds nothing good from us, even trials, pain and suffering which are at work in our lives to become stronger, wiser and more holy. God in His Greatness is able to turn around everything and make it good, to those who love Him and called to His purposes (Romans 8:28). Let us reflect again the final promise in David's psalm, *Surely His Goodness and Mercy shall follow me all the days of my life; and I will dwell in the house of the LORD Forever* (23:6).

CHAPTER 5

The Grace of God

Grace may be said to be the greatest most wonderful gift by God to
mankind, paid for with the greatest price in the universe, and given
freely to those who least deserve it.

*For it is by grace you have been saved, through faith—and this is not from yourselves,
it is the gift of God—not by works, so that no one can boast. For we are God's
handiwork, created in Christ Jesus to do good works, God prepared in advance for us
to do.*
—Ephesians 2:8-10 NIV

*E*verything had been prepared, including the expensive wedding ring. Months before
the wedding, the bride and the groom-to-be planned a great reception. The couple had
gone to the Hyatt Hotel in downtown Boston and painstakingly picked out the menu,
the china and silver, and even the flower arrangements that they liked. The bill came
to $13,000, and for something like that, they had to leave a 50% down payment.

The next few months were spent on ironing out the remaining one thousand and
one details: the immaculately-white wedding cake, the limousine, and of course,
last-minute finishing touches on the wedding gown. Everyone was so excited. Then
the day the invitations were about to be sent out, the groom-to-be suddenly got cold
feet and told his fiancée that he really wasn't sure if he was ready. To make a long story
short, the wedding was cancelled, and the woman, our potential bride, as expected,
was upset.

To make matters worse, her ex-fiancé disappeared altogether from the scene, leaving her the painful task of canceling all previous arrangements, including the wedding party. As if things were not bad enough, when she went to the Hyatt to cancel the reception, the Events Manager shook her head sympathetically and told her, "The contract is binding. You're only entitled to $1,300 back. You have two options: to forfeit the rest of the down payment, or go ahead with the banquet. I'm sorry."

Guess what the bride decided to do? She decided to go ahead with the party—not a wedding party, of course, but a big blow-out. She had the wild notion of inviting not only her family and friends, but all the poor, homeless and disadvantaged of Boston! So she invited the aging from the nursing homes. She sent out invitations to rescue missions and homeless shelters. Her friends thought she had gone out of her mind. "Are you crazy?" they told her, "throwing a party that's free for all?!" "Yup," she quipped, "all in honour of the groom."

And so in June of 1990, the Hyatt Hotel in downtown Boston hosted a party unlike any other held there before. The homeless came; the elderly were wheeled in from their nursing homes. People who were used to picking up half-gnawed pizza from bins feasted instead on chicken cordon bleu. Hyatt waiters in tuxedos served champagne to senior citizens in wheelchairs and aluminum walkers. Bag ladies, drug addicts, and beggars took the night off from the streets of downtown Boston, relished the wedding cake, and danced long into the night. It was the most unusual wedding party of all . . . [1]

The doctrine of Grace is an essential teaching which many people do not fully understand or properly appreciate. Its true meaning and application are still very much a mystery today. Grace is often defined as *approval, pardon, privilege* and *favour.*[2] It is a gift that one does not receive by any means but out of the kindness of the giver. It is the combination of God's Goodness, Love, Mercy towards all people without regard to their past sins and offences.

Jesus spoke to them again in parables, saying: "The kingdom of heaven is like a king who prepared a wedding banquet for his son. He sent his servants to those who had been invited to the banquet to tell them to come . . ."

—Matthew 22:1-3 NIV

Grace is best represented in the form of a feast. A feast represents abundance, nourishment to the body; at a cost to the giver; free of charge; on the house and no strings attached. To those who do not deserve it, and who can never repay them back. Just like the story of the bride who invited the poor, the elderly, and the homeless to the wedding feast, her extravagant generosity to people she did not know and did not have the ability to pay back is *true grace* in action. Not surprisingly, Jesus' parables are filled with grace. Workers receiving the same pay for a full day's work; the parable of the lost son; the woman at the well; and the woman caught in adultery. All stories of *exaggerated* grace. And that was the point.

The word grace appears in the Old Testament 38 times, while in the New Testament it appears a staggering 128 times. Clearly, the work of the Cross has tripled in its significance towards God and all mankind. 1 John 2:1-2 says, *My dear children, I am writing this to you so that you will not sin. But if anyone does sin, we have an advocate who pleads our case before the Father. He is Jesus Christ, the one who is truly righteous. He himself is the sacrifice that atones for our sins—and not only our sins but the sins of all the world.*

Ephesians 2:8 says, *For it is by grace you have been saved, through faith—and this is not from yourselves, it is the gift of God—not by works, so that no one can boast.* Here we see an essential truth. We are not saved by good works but for good works. All people are on the same level, none can boast that they achieved salvation by their own means. As we move toward spiritual maturity, we become more aware of our sinfulness; and the more aware we are of God's Grace to forgive and show kindness to us daily. God will receive all the glory for all eternity by all the redeemed, forever and ever. Such is the power of His Grace.

Salvation is God's idea and by His terms. By His *Grace*, through your *faith*, you now have salvation and your sins are forgiven. God's Grace is a free gift that can not be earned on our part by any means. It is solely based on the work of the cross, with God's judgement towards mankind falling on Jesus in our place. No matter how godly you are or close to perfection, salvation is only at God's freedom to do so. It is impossible to be saved apart from Grace. It is just as impossible without faith. If Grace is the door, faith is the key that unlocks its treasures.

Amazing Grace

John Newton was an unforgiving slave trader in the 1700s. His human African cargo were viewed as possessions, not people. They were chained below decks, starved and any of them stricken with smallpox or disease were cast overboard to drown. Consistent mortality rates of most slave trader vessels were a staggering 20-25 percent.

The turning point in Newton's life occurred when a violent storm happened during a standard trip at sea. Moments after he left the deck, the crewman who had taken his place was swept overboard to his death. He later realised his helplessness and concluded that only the Grace of God could save him. On a homeward voyage while he was attempting to steer the ship through a separate violent storm, he experienced what he was to refer to later as his 'great deliverance'. He recorded in his journal that when all seemed lost and the ship would surely sink, he exclaimed, '*Lord, have mercy on us.*' Later in his cabin he reflected on what he had said and began to believe that God had saved his life and his crew. Grace had begun to work within him.

These incidents and his 1750 marriage to Mary Cartlett changed Newton significantly. Later on his slave voyages, he encouraged the sailors under his charge to pray. He also began to ensure that every member of his crew treated their human cargo with gentleness and concern. Nevertheless, it would be another forty years until Newton openly challenged the trafficking of slave's altogether.[3] He eventually left the trade and was moved to go into ministry. For the last forty-three years of his life preached the gospel in London. At eighty-two, Newton said, "*My memory is nearly gone, but I remember two things; that I am a great sinner, and that Christ is a great Saviour.*" It was from this understanding and revelation that he famously penned these words:

Amazing grace, how sweet the sound,
That saved a wretch like me.
I once was lost, but now am found,
Was blind but now I see.
My chains are gone, I've been set free,
My God My Saviour, has ransomed me.
And like a flood, His mercy reigns,
Unending love, Amazing Grace.

Newton's hymn vividly sums up God's Grace towards all humanity. The song has become known as a favourite with supporters of freedom and human rights, both Christian and non-Christian. John Newton understood the Grace of God in his lifetime. How much more should we?

The Nature of God is to Show Grace

> *Rejoice, you people of Jerusalem! Rejoice in the LORD your God! For the rain he sends demonstrates his faithfulness. Once more the autumn rains will come, as well as the rains of spring. The threshing floors will again be piled high with grain, and the presses will overflow with new wine and olive oil.*
> —Joel 2:23-24 NLT

God's Grace is solely based on His nature which is to show us divine Mercy and Goodness to lead us to repentance. It is not by our own merit, ability, good works, special knowledge, faith, or gifting's. God is no respecter of persons. He is Good to all men in His common Grace, pouring out daily blessings on the wicked and the righteous alike. Specifically, we can see there are two types of God's Grace:

1) Common Grace—the Goodness of God given to all people, good and bad, righteous and unrighteous—the gift of life, rain, sunshine (Joel 2:23, Matthew 5:45);

2) Saving Grace—the undeserved favour, forgiveness, mercy and salvation freely given as a gift to those who believe and obey by faith (Ephesians 2:8-9).

We are justified by His Grace, getting what we don't deserve and instead receiving every blessing, favour and kindness imaginable. We will share in Heaven as heirs of Christ, adopted as children into God's family. With this understanding we live in constant hope that looks beyond the concerns of this life. Where there is no hope, we must have hope.

Through Adam's fall and sin we have been *dis-graced* and separated from God. But in Christ's obedience and sacrifice, we have been *restored* to Grace and reconciled. Jesus came in Grace and Truth (John 1:17). A standard of expectation was required, but if failed, there was grace to forgive and to restore.

> *One of the criminals who hung there hurled insults at him: "Aren't you the Christ? Save yourself and us!" But the other criminal rebuked him. "Don't you fear God," he said, "since you are under the same sentence? We are punished justly, for we are getting what our deeds deserve. But this man has done nothing wrong." Then he said, "Jesus, remember me when you come into your kingdom." Jesus answered him, "I tell you the truth, today you will be with me in paradise."*
> —Luke 23:39-43 NIV

There is arguably no better illustration of Jesus' life of giving Grace to others in need than the story of the two criminals on the Cross. It also shows just how personal and astounding Grace is which the world struggles to accept. Grace doesn't make sense to those who don't know God. True Grace is in all honesty shockingly personal. In a way it is entirely unfair and unwarranted. However, God's Grace is not about fairness but unconditional love mixed with forgiveness, liberation and reconciliation.

The story of the two criminals next to Jesus on the Cross is an incredible narrative. Firstly, to die by crucifixion was for the worst of the worst of criminals. It was a public example to all those who observed travelling in and out of the city that any form of rebellion against the Roman Empire would be punished. In Jesus last dying hours on earth, He still cared about the two dying men next to Him. The first criminal wanted Jesus to do something for him. To prove His authority as the Christ and set Himself and both of them free. But the second criminal wanted to do something for Jesus. To forgive him of his sins and come into His Kingdom. Both were equally close to Jesus. One repented, the other didn't. Jesus loved the repentant thief to grant him paradise. And Jesus loved the unrepentant thief to allow him the free choice not to.

This unknown repented criminal was the first person to receive the full Grace of Jesus Christ by the work of the Cross. What is clear is he didn't do anything deserving of Grace. He lived a life of crime and sin. He wasn't baptised or faithfully attend church. He didn't give extravagant offerings or serve sacrificially at church. And it is doubtful he did any good works. Yet Jesus gave him salvation at the dying moments of his life. This Grace is not surprisingly difficult for most people to understand. It means to forgive the unforgivable and to love the unlovable. It is not something you can earn or purchase, it is a gift given freely. To be a Christian means to forgive the inexcusable, because God has forgiven the inexcusable in us. Grace may be said to be the greatest most wonderful gift by God to mankind, paid for with the greatest price in the universe, and given freely to those who least deserve it. Truly, truly, Amazing Grace.

'By the Grace of God, I am what I am . . .'

> *[As God's fellow workers] with Him then, we beg of you not to receive the grace of God in vain [the merciful kindness by which <u>God exerts His holy influence on souls</u> and <u>turns them into Christ</u>] . . .*
> —2 Corinthians 6:1 AMP, author's emphasis

The New Testament reveals that God's Grace plays a central part in man's redemption. Specifically, Grace consists of a number of important qualities available to us today. These include:

1) Undeserved Kindness—compassion and mercy
2) Forgiveness—pardon of sins and transgressions
3) Salvation—eternity in heaven in God's presence
4) Empowerment—the ability to live righteously in the power of the Holy Spirit

Grace is God's undeserved kindness, the forgiveness of sins and eternal salvation. However, it must be emphasised that the primary functional purpose of the gift of God's Grace is *empowerment*. Strong defines Grace as *the divine influence upon the heart and its reflection in the life*.[4] It is also the unmerited divine assistance given man for his regeneration or sanctification. Grace is an invisible power and influence living in the mind, body and spirit of a surrendered life.

Every step of faith should be one step closer to losing your life. The more of you, you lose, the more of Christ's life you gain. The life your losing is not the life you want anyway—IN Christ is the real you—who God created. God's version of you is the Ferrari version of you—IN Christ.
—Bill Johnson, Senior Pastor Bethel Church in Redding, California[5]

Paul emphasised this influence and power of Grace in his letters often. Titus 2:11-12 says, *For the grace of God that brings salvation has appeared to all men, teaching us that, denying ungodliness and worldly lusts, we should live soberly, righteously, and godly in the present age.* One of the clearest statements on the operation of grace is found here. It is the invisible power of God that transforms the life and heart of the individual, causing the believer to turn away from ungodliness and worldly lusts and to live righteously. Grace brings salvation, but it does not stop there. It continues to operate, teaching and training the Christian how to live a life that stands in sharp contrast to his former life. It teaches us to live a totally different life; *soberly, righteously, and godly.*

By the grace of God I am what I am: and his grace which was bestowed upon me was not in vain; but I laboured more abundantly than they all: yet not I, but the grace of God which was with me.
—1 Corinthians 15:10 NIV

Before Paul was converted he was a zealous violent Pharisee, on the way to imprison and kill followers of Jesus. But on the dusty roads of Damascus, he had a physical encounter of the resurrected Christ and was changed forever. Years later, Paul could rightly say of himself, *By the grace of God I am what I am*. The transforming power of grace working within Paul over the years was now an entirely different person. Paul always greeted and wished his readers grace in all of his letters. Not an empty promise but a reality. It was the best gift he himself had received and the best gift he could give to others.

Before I came to Christ, I was a worldly, selfish and angry young man. Coming from a broken home, all I knew was pain and had to fight my way through life to get my rights. I would swear frequently horrible words to anyone who upset me. One such character flaw was being incredibly greedy with money. I remember once stopping at McDonald's on the way home from primary school and ordering a $4.95 meal. A few moments after sitting down, an older boy came up to me needing five cents to pay for his meal. Seeing the five cents on my tray he asked if he could have it. I flatly said 'No' in no uncertain terms and told him to get it from someone else. How unbelievable!

However, after surrendering my life to Christ I am now one of the most giving people around. In my first years as a believer, I shouted dozens of meals to friends, gave regularly to church and sacrificed financially and materially to family, friends and strangers, saved and unsaved. I lived to give and would even go out of my way to help others unexpectantly. The transformation was sudden and surprised everyone close to me. It does not stop there. Each year I see an improved change in my words, actions and mindsets. I am no longer a worldly, selfish and angry young man anymore. Just like Paul, I can rightly say of myself: *By the Grace of God I am what I am*!

Acts 11:22-24 says, *The report of this came to the ears of the church in Jerusalem, and they sent Barnabas to Antioch. <u>When he came and saw the grace of God, he was glad,</u> and he exhorted them all to remain faithful to the Lord with steadfast purpose, for he was a good man, full of the Holy Spirit and of faith. And a great many people were added to the Lord* (author's emphasis). The evidence of a changed life is the greatest evidence of a real and powerful God. Here we see that when Barnabas saw the Christians of Antioch, he could tangibly see the Grace of God had brought about a transformation. They were renewed and sanctified to live lives that honoured God and reflected the love and nature of Christ. They were *empowered* to live His ways and to walk in His precepts of holiness and righteousness.

This is the power of God's *transforming, renewing, sanctifying* and *empowering* Grace. It is available to you today if you genuinely choose it and take it with both hands. Remember: it is a *power* given to you to live the life God's laws previously demanded we must live by. It is similar to using the escalator at an airport instead of the stairs. Why use the effort to reach the top when there is a free option available to get there without the energy? Like driving a car from one city to another. Though you are making no effort physically, you are being transported naturally by the vehicle. The enemy to receiving God's Grace is pride. James 4:6 says, *For God opposes the proud but* He *gives grace to the humble.* Pride keeps you far from God, but humility keeps you close.

Old Testament Grace consisted of mostly God's undeserved kindness. New Testament grace is however so much more. It is His transforming, renewing, sanctifying and empowering Grace to every believer who desires and seeks it diligently. God did not want mankind to be bound by religion and works only to be saved and be bound by sin and lawlessness. In Christ we have abundant freedom and liberty to live for Him until the end of the age (Galatians 5:1).

And God is able to make all grace abound to you, so that in all things at all times, having all that you need, you will abound in every good work.
—2 Corinthians 9:8 NIV, author's emphasis

The power of God's empowering Grace is available at every opportunity in life. Grace is imparted supernaturally:

1. *All things* = family and friends, work, study, ministry, serving.
2. *All times* = in lack, need, abundance, want, in conflict, in peace.
3. *All that you need* = finances, wisdom, strength, peace, joy, hope, faith.

Grace for strength in a time of weakness, wisdom in a time of uncertainty. Grace to have faith, hope and love in a time of hopelessness and emptiness. Most importantly, no matter how deeply you have been immersed in sin, by faith in the name of Jesus, you have access through His imputed righteousness to the *changing power* of God's Grace to become holy and set free. Our response to receive this gift, is to seek Him in prayer, read His Word, and to work in co-operation with the Holy Spirit. *Where sin abounds, grace abounds even more* when this is our true heart's desire (Romans 5:20). For we are dead to sin and alive to Christ in His abundant Grace!

> *Even though I have received such wonderful revelations from God to keep me from becoming proud, I was given a thorn in my flesh . . . three different times I begged the Lord to take it away. Each time he said, "My grace is sufficient for you. My power works best in weakness." So now I am glad to boast about my weaknesses, so that the power of Christ can work through me . . .*
> —2 Corinthians 12:7-9 NLT, author's emphasis

Additionally, another important area of Grace is that it works best in our weaknesses. To keep Paul from becoming prideful he had what most agree to be a deterorating health condition (Galatians 4:13-15). This was clearly a serious problem for him to pray about it three times on different occasions. Being involved in church planting, he could not afford to let anything get in the way of his presentation of the gospel. However, he had to learn that his human nature, having experienced incredible revelations from heaven, was to become prideful and self-righteous, much like ours today.

Our weaknesses can be varied and different to most people around us. It may be a struggle to forgive a family member or person in leadership, to stay free from anger and powerful emotions, or to be generous and be giving to those in need. It can also be character flaws of low self-confidence, sexual immorality, or lifestyle addictions of alcohol, drugs, gambling and promiscuity.

Friend, God wants to turn your weaknesses and struggles into your greatest strengths. Everyday people are watching you and relying on you to be strong in life. Your breakthrough will be an example and inspiration for others who are going through the same issues. There is another person on the other side of your victory! No matter how difficult, embarrassing or impossible your weaknesses, God's *transforming, renewing, sanctifying* and *empowering* Grace is sufficient for you. God is a Redeemer and He desires to restore every broken area of your life. It may not happen overnight or in a year, but eventually you will experience breakthrough living a life of surrender, humility, perseverance and faith in your Redeemer. By trusting in Him, gradual change and transformation are worth the wait!

Grace + Truth = Jesus Christ

And of His fullness we have all received—Grace upon Grace. For the law was given through Moses but Grace and Truth came through Jesus Christ.
—John 1:16-17 ESV, author's emphasis

In the Old Testament, all people lived under the Law of Moses. To disobey God's laws and sin was to require an animal sacrifice to atone for that sin. However, when Jesus came to earth everything changed. Before Grace there was expectation to live and obey all the requirements of the law and endless sacrifices. But with Grace we are now free from the law and have the ability to obey His commands ourselves. We are no longer under the curse of the law but now under the freedom to live righteously in Grace!

The Apostle John writes, *In the beginning was the Word, and the Word was with God and the Word was God* (John 1:1). Jesus was the fulfillment of all Old Testament prophecies and the Law of Moses. He lived a perfect life without sin and willingly took the place of punishment on behalf of sinful mankind. Jesus was the Word of God in physical from. Jesus was with God and was God, being one expression of the Trinity. John writes, *The Word became flesh and made his dwelling among us. We have seen his glory, the glory of the One and Only, who came from the Father, full of grace and truth* (John 1:14).

To say that Jesus dwelt among them literally meant to live with them; to eat, drink, sleep and do everyday tasks with them daily for years. They saw Him with their eyes, looked upon Him, and their hands handled Him. He was with them as a friend and as one of a family, so that they had full opportunity of becoming familiarly acquainted with Him, to the point where He could not be mistaken.[6] Jesus came in Grace and Truth. He was kind, merciful, gracious, doing good to all, and seeking man's best welfare by great sacrifices and love. And He declared the Truth; in Him was no falsehood. He was not like the false prophets and false Messiahs who were impostors; but He was Truth itself. He represented things as they are, and thus became the truth as well as the way and the life.[7]

> Let us then _approach the throne of grace with confidence,_
> so that we may receive mercy and _find grace_ to help us in our time of need.
> —Hebrews 4:16 NIV, author's emphasis

Furthermore, Jesus, our Great High Priest, pleads for our case. We may come before God with boldness and look for pardon. We come not depending on our own merits, but we come where a sufficient sacrifice has been offered for human guilt, and where we are assured that God is merciful. We come without hesitation or trembling, but simply ask to receive mercy and find grace in our time of need.

The King of the universe rules with kindness, compassion, mercy and forgiveness. Mercy and grace are the two things we always need. Mercy to forgive our sins, and Grace to purify our souls. We are invited to come boldly in our times of weakness and struggles. If we are invited to come to Him, it means He is approachable and available at all times. We are to come confidently and with childlike faith. Never arrogantly and prideful. We are to fully trust in His judgements for our life. This is a glimpse of what Heaven looks like. God rules a Kingdom righteously executing it with justice and fairness. This is the God that I serve. This is the God I surrender my life too. This is the Greatness of our God!

The False Gospel of Grace—A Word of Warning

[As God's fellow workers] with Him then, we beg of you not to receive the grace of
God in vain [the merciful kindness by which God exerts His holy influence on souls
and turns them into Christ] . . .

—2 Corinthians 6:1 AMP, author's emphasis

Now, when I first became saved at seventeen, a few others started the race at the same time as me. One such friend committed his life a few years earlier and came from a tough upbringing. Regularly I would help him with lifts during the week, shout meals, and encourage him in life and the faith. He came into my men's study group and I discipled him. However, year after year would go by and there would be no change in his behaviour. He loved the social aspect of church life but resisted personal change and working on areas he needed to deal with.

Finally after five years I became frustrated. I had gone above and beyond helping him but there was never any sign of improvement or change. He loved the party lifestyle of drinking and smoking more than anything. Because he received government paychecks he had no intention of finding work or study. Instead he played computer games all week and would sleep in till 3:00pm. Eventually, he soon left church and now no longer attends. He lives a defeated life and blames everyone for his problems. Furthermore, he claims to still be a 'Christian' while justifying his behaviour as *'It's okay, I'm under grace'*.

Why is it that some people can go to church for five to ten years but never change? Why are some still the same annoying, selfish, bad mouthed, hot-tempered people twenty years later? Spiritual maturity is sadly missing in many churches because failure in the pursuit of it has caused us to settle for less. There are at least four common reasons why Christians refuse to become mature in Christ:

1) **Minimum Christianity**—only want to just get into Heaven, 'Sunday Christian'

2) **Laziness and Apathy**—'drifters', no interest in proceeding further in their walk with God

3) **Sin and Disobedience**—habitual lifestyle of sin and unrepentance, still own their life

4) **Held back from the past**—unforgiveness, bitterness, anger, offences etc.

I often ask myself, '*As a Christian people should see a significant difference in my life*'. Think about it: the closer I am to God, the more I should become like Him. There should be a major change on the inside of me, including my heart, mind, motivations, desires, beliefs and values. All of these should change the outside and the visible—our actions, words, deeds. Ultimately, we must ask ourselves regularly: Is there evidence of a changed life? Is there fruit of repentance? Are there signs of transformation in behaviour? Paul wrote, *we beg of you not to receive the grace of God in vain*. Notice the tone in his words. He pleads for us to take great caution. Clearly we can miss the Grace of God which is a very dangerous place to be.

Paul, realising that Grace could be misunderstood, explained its implication in Romans, *Well then, should we keep on sinning so that God can show us more and more of his wonderful grace? Of course not! Since we have died to sin, how can we continue to live in it? Or have you forgotten that when we were joined with Christ Jesus in baptism, we joined him in his death? For we died and were buried with Christ by baptism. And just as Christ was raised from the dead by the glorious power of the Father, now we also may live new lives* (6:1-4). Paul's argument is simple: if we have been set free from the slavery of sin which we were bound in the sinful nature, why would we continue to live in it? A life of freedom and victory awaits us!

> *Examine yourselves as to whether you are in the faith. Test yourselves. Do you not know yourselves, that Jesus Christ is in you?—unless indeed you are disqualified.*
> —2 Corinthians 13:5 NKJV

To be disqualified is to be counterfeit, unapproved, and failing the test. In contrast, to be approved is to be qualified and genuine. *Behaviour never lies*. Our thoughts, words and actions speak the loudest at the end of the day. Christians who live in deliberate sin are deceived of their true nature and always believe they are right.

They refuse to change and live in darkness. When the light is shined on them their true nature comes out, which is always an alarming sight to see!

With this amazing Grace comes a great responsibility for us to use it properly. Scripture is clear that the wonderful grace of God is not to be abused. Jude 3-4 says, *Dear friends, I had been eagerly planning to write to you about the salvation we all share. But now I find that I must write about something else, <u>urging you to defend the faith</u> that God has entrusted once for all time to his holy people. I say this because some ungodly people have wormed their way into your churches, <u>saying that God's marvelous grace allows us to live immoral lives</u>. The condemnation of such people was recorded long ago, for they have denied our only Master and Lord, Jesus Christ* (author's emphasis). It is clear: those who use God's forgiveness to live immoral lives will be brought to ruin. God's marvelous Grace is not be abused. For God can not be mocked. He can not be tamed, but He will surely tame the unruly Christian.

The purpose of God's Grace is so our heart and mind would be totally transformed and empowered to *live* for Christ, to build the Kingdom of God. Salvations price is sacrifice of self and the death of your sinful nature. True Grace is not salvation, but instead a *process* on our part that brings salvation. All who abuse this doctrine of Grace are without excuse. Grace is free, salvation is not free. Read the bible.

For the world would love to have a Christ to excuse them, at no cost, to continue to live in their sins, passions and evil desires. There's will be everlasting separation from God in torment and darkness. But, to those who are committed to Truth, they would have a Christ to change them to live a life well pleasing to God, whatever the cost.
                                                                              —Anonymous

Grace's Contemporary: God's Cursings

However, if you do not obey the LORD your God and do not carefully follow all his commands . . . all these curses will come on you and overtake you: You will be <u>cursed in the city and cursed in the country</u>. Your <u>basket and your kneading trough will be cursed. The fruit of your womb will be cursed</u>, and the crops of your land, and the calves of your herds and the lambs of your flocks. You will be <u>cursed when you</u>

come in and cursed when you go out. The LORD will send on you curses, confusion and rebuke in everything you put your hand to, until you are destroyed and come to sudden ruin because of the evil you have done in forsaking Him.
—Deuteronomy 28:15-20 NIV, author's emphasis

God has set before all humanity the option to choose blessings or curses, life and death. Joshua 24:15 says, . . . *choose for yourselves this day whom you will serve.* It is up to us to choose at the end of the day. We can still be a child of God and cursed at the same time because of deliberate, unconfessed sin. Curses are a temporary law of the universe resulting from sin, but if not dealt with will lead to God's permanent Judgement.

A blessing or curse is essentially an unseen spiritual reality operating daily in a person's life. You are either under the covering of the curse of the law, or free and under Grace. Deuteronomy 28:15-20 explains in detail the life of an individual when living under the curse of the law. They are cursed in travelling, cursed in work, career, assets, and finances, cursed in reproduction, and cursed in life! The planets align against you and there is nothing you can do to prevent it! The primary reasons for curses come from disobedience and sin. The seven generic curses can be summarised as:

1) **Humiliation**—embarrassment and shame from friends, family, co-workers, strangers;
2) **Barrenness**—infertility and unfruitfulness physically and spiritually; no legacy;
3) **Sickness**—bad health, diseases and infirmities of any kind;
4) **Poverty**—fail financially, emotionally, materially; constant struggling and effort to succeed;
5) **Defeat**—relentless setbacks in work leisure; lives a defeated life;
6) **The tail and not the head**—at the end of lines, ignored, taken advantage of, manipulated;
7) **Below and not above in life**—remembers the challenges of the past, pessimistic, negative outlook on life, difficult to rise above challenges, missed opportunities.

I read a story recently that really highlighted this unseen spiritual reality. A British couple living together travelled on a holiday to the Maldives. On the third day of their exclusive beach resort, they were accused of stealing $600 from their neighbouring bungalow which was found in their bathroom drawer. Being an all-inclusive resort they had no idea how it got there. The local police were called and the aggrieved family began to make them feel exceptionally uncomfortable, taking photographs and video footage of them. The police presence on the island continued and the couple were fingerprinted and asked to give multiple statements. The whole experience shook them greatly.

But it didn't end there. The police demanded they be taken by boat to the capital Male to be interrogated. Due to inconsistencies in their stories they were arrested on suspicion of theft and needed to hire a lawyer at a cost of $4,000. They were sent to a detention centre and then transported to an island prison to be incarcerated until their court case could be heard. After being photographed, stripped of all possessions and strip searched for drugs, they were thrown into separate prison cells, eaten alive by mosquitoes. Desperate requests to speak to their lawyer were ignored. Several days later they were handcuffed and taken by boat with some fifty other inmates and under heavy guard.

Terrified, exhausted and bewildered they were led by police to a courthouse in Male. The trial was spoken at great length in a foreign language. Worst case scenario the judge could have ruled a three year gaol term, but let them off confiscating their passports. The whole ordeal had torn apart their lives and family members back at home. To date, no compensation or explanation was given.[8]

No matter how happy you might be living a life of sin, you can never find lasting happiness under the curse of the law. This is not the life you and I were meant to live. God takes no pleasure in seeing His people in pain, suffering, sickness or poverty. We choose our destiny and must take full responsibility for our behaviour and decisions.

[But] if you fully obey the LORD your God and carefully follow all his commands I give you today, the LORD your God will set you high above all the nations on earth.

All these blessings will come upon you and accompany you if you obey the LORD your God: You will be <u>blessed in the city and blessed in the country</u>. The <u>fruit of your womb will be blessed</u>, and the <u>crops of your land and the young of your livestock</u>—the calves of your herds and the lambs of your flocks. Your <u>basket and your kneading trough will be blessed</u>. You will be <u>blessed when you come in and blessed when you go out</u>. The LORD will grant that the enemies who rise up against you will be defeated before you. They will come at you from one direction but flee from you in seven. The LORD will send a blessing on your barns and on everything you put your hand to . . . The LORD will make you the head, not the tail. If you pay attention to the commands of the LORD your God that I give you this day and carefully follow them, you will always be at the top, never at the bottom.
—Deuteronomy 28:1-8; 13 NIV, author's emphasis

However, take heart. Cursings can be lifted once true repentance has taken place, which is a change of heart and lifestyle. Here we see that all of the curses of the law are reversed when our life honours God and we live in obedience to all of His ways. The seven generic blessings include:

1) **Exaltation**—praise and honour from friends, family, co-workers, strangers;

2) **Reproduction**—healthy fertility and fruitfulness in offspring, physically and spiritually legacy;

3) **Good Health**—physical health strong, fit, relaxed, total well-being, peace with self and others;

4) **Prosperity**—successful financially, emotionally, materially, affluent;

5) **Victory**—triumphant in work and leisure, a winner in life;

6) **The head and not the tail**—favour follows you wherever you go, first in, best dressed, recommended the best and cheapest when shopping instead of the overpriced counterfeit;

7) **Above and not beneath in life**—strong, happy and healthy in life, optimistic and confident in the future, uses mistakes as stepping stones to promotion and success!

This is the life you and I were meant to live. All the planets align in your favour. You are blessed when you walk in and blessed when you walk out. Everywhere you go you are living under an open heaven and no one knows why! God takes great joy when we are living a life that pleases Him. *Therefore we make it our aim, whether present or absent, to be well pleasing to Him* (2 Corinthians 5:9).

Example—Numbers 22: Balaam and Israel

After four hundred years of slavery, the Israelites are led out of Egypt by Moses. After an incredible encounter with God at Mount Sinai they head towards the Promised Land. On the way they approach the land of Moab which God has already promised them victory over:

> *So Balak, who was king of Moab, sent messengers to summon Balaam . . . and said: "A people has come out of Egypt; they cover the face of the land and have settled next to me. Now come and put a curse on these people, because they are too powerful for me. Perhaps then I will be able to defeat them and drive them out of the land. For I know that whoever you bless is blessed, and whoever you curse is cursed." . . . But God said to Balaam, "Do not go with them. You must not put a curse on those people, because they are blessed."*
> —Numbers 22:4-6; 12 NIV, author's emphasis

Firstly, the enemy can't curse what God has blessed! God has the last say at the end of the day. He is always in control in His sovereignty. Furthermore, the devil has been defeated at the Cross of Calvary for 2,000 years and has no power or authority over the life of a born again believer. Balaam later disobeys God's voice and goes up to the mountain where Israel is camped. However, even in disobedience God still used him to speak a number of blessings over them instead.:

> *How can I curse those whom God has not cursed? . . . From the rocky peaks I see them, from the heights I view them. I see a people who live apart and do not consider themselves one of the nations. Who can count the dust of Jacob or number even a fourth of Israel? Let me die the death of the righteous, and may my final end be like theirs!*
> —Numbers 23:8-10 NIV

This is an incredible prophecy of God's people by a pagan who had no covenant or even remote understanding of God. Balaam speaks of great praise and honour of God's people and how greatly they are blessed! He admits publically that:

i) God's people are set apart and not of this world
ii) Their descendants are like sand on the sea shore, too many to count
iii) Proclaimed they were righteous and desired to even die like them!

As Christian's we are to be the most blessed and successful people on planet earth. We are to be the hardest working, faithful and anointed in our families and communities. We are the light of the world. We hold the answers for the world's problems. We are the righteousness of Christ. People should be running to churches weekly when they see that the secret to our success is our relationship with God! This was His intention before the beginning of creation.

Sadly, Balaam's greed for money and honour was greater than his encounter with God. He later advised King Balak how Israel could be cursed—self-inflicted sin through temptation, feasting, idol worship and sexual immorality (see Numbers 25). Believers can come back under the curse of the law by wickedness and sin. Later on, the men of Israel feasted, worshipped false god's and slept with the idolatrous women causing the Lord's anger to blaze against His people. Twenty-two thousand died in one day and Judgement fell. The greatest challenge Israel had to face was not the hostile armies of foreign lands but the constant temptations to compromise their faith in God. Despite being blessed miraculously and abundantly, they chose evil and wickedness which opened the door for God's curses to come upon them.

We are no different today. The world has just as many temptations and evil available within our reach. There are more options today and lesser standards than at any other time in history. Technology, the internet and the availability of alcohol, drugs, sexual immorality and many others are everywhere. In the midst of temptation don't turn your back on God, turn your back on the world. Let this be a warning to all of us so as not to repeat Israel's mistakes, but instead pursue Grace in our time of need.

Final Thoughts

Our faith, conversion and eternal salvation are all the free gift of God's Grace. It was His purpose from the beginning which He prepared for us, blessing us with the knowledge of His will, made possible by the power of the Holy Spirit. This is a true doctrine and will continue to be the only way of salvation until the end of the world.

A word of encouragement: If you're struggling with sin, His *Grace* is sufficient. If you're going through a storm, His *Grace* is sufficient. If you're fighting the enemy and you feel like you can't win, His *Grace* is sufficient. If you're praying for a breakthrough, His *Grace* is sufficient! The power of God's transforming, renewing, sanctifying and empowering Grace is available to you today. He sees you as a finished product. No matter what you are going through this Grace is enough for you to get through this season.

Therefore, I challenge you, be eager to forgive, delight to show mercy, take joy in reconciling with those who have wronged you. Go up to someone today that there is tension or unresolved unforgiveness between and tell them how much you love them—all because of the amazing and generous Grace that has been poured out to you. Truly, truly, Amazing Grace!

CHAPTER 6

The Love of God

God' Love triumphs over all wickedness, overlooking a person's past
and instead looking at the individual's potential good.

This is how God showed His love among us: He sent His one and only Son into the world that we might live through Him. <u>This is love: not that we loved God, but that He loved us and sent His Son as an atoning sacrifice for our sins.</u> Dear friends, since God so loved us, we also ought to love one another. No one has ever seen God; but if we love one another, God lives in us and His love is made complete in us.
—1 John 4:9-12 NIV, author's emphasis

In 1981 the FBI was on the lookout for one of the Top Ten Most Wanted Men, Stephen Marin, a murderer and rapist, prowling San Antonio, Texas. He was brought up in a broken family and learned to hate women. He built and maintained this resentment in his childhood which later turned to violence. He was now on the run after murdering a waitress and avoiding authorities.

Looking for one more victim he came upon Margie Mayfield, a wife, mother, and strong woman of faith. Armed with a revolver he abducted her in a shopping centre car park and drove off in her van down the dark highway. He told her to sit on her hands in the passenger seat and not do or say anything or he would kill her.

Margie remained calm and prayed silently to herself with her eyes closed. Though she knew full well who he was, she repeated in her thoughts "Perfect love casts out fear" over and over. After a few minutes he looked at her and asked why she wasn't afraid. She said "Because God put me in this car with you for a reason".

She spoke to Stephen in a mother-to-son tone and said to him "Do you know Jesus Christ? He came for you, to save you from sins and eternal death". To Stephen, no one had ever cared about him before or spoken to him about the gospel. In all his anger and life of crime he rarely thought of God. Margie continued, "You are living in a prison Stephen, Christ can set you free. God loves you and you are known to Him. He is your Father in heaven and is knocking on the door of your heart". Her softness and approachability spoke to this hardened man and he pondered and listened to her words.

Whilst he drove her mobile called. It was her husband who was concerned why she wasn't home, worried she might be in danger, being in the area of the last murder by this serial killer. She told him calmly she would be home later and hanged up! She later told him and the authorities that she did this as she felt 100% safe because the presence of God was in her van.

They drove around some more, parked the van and talked. She said "No matter what you've done Stephen—anything—the power of Christ's blood is more powerful. For God so loved Stephen Marin that He gave His only Son, that if Stephen Marin believes in Him he will not perish but have eternal life". She said he must be born again and explained how he had been born by his earthly father, by earthly seed; but now he must be born of spiritual seed, of the Heavenly Father.

After a short time amazingly he emptied his bullets into her purse! After a few hours he surrendered his will and his life to God. Eventually, after more discussion about Jesus, conversion and Christian life, he spontaneously raised his arms toward the sky, saying: "Lord, I'm sorry for all I've done; please forgive me". He was a changed man. They then drove toward their next stop for Stephen to catch a bus. They spoke final words and as they departed this once-crazed-killer cried like a baby on her shoulder.

Later the FBI later called her at home and Margie, somewhat reluctantly for fear of a shootout, told them where he was: in a bus station reading a bible she gave him. They didn't believe her: a Ten Top Most Wanted man, sitting in a bus station, reading a bible? Come on! But sure enough: when they went there, there he was, sitting peacefully reading the bible at Psalm 119:105: "Your word is a lamp unto my feet and a light unto my path". Unknown to Margie he had more bullets in his pockets. But when they approached him Stephen said to them: "I met this lady today. She changed my life. If I didn't I would have killed you all and then killed myself"... [1]

Firstly, in case you are asking 'Hugh, why didn't you talk about God's Love first? That is the first chapter everyone wants to read and what everyone knows about'. My answer is we can't properly understand God's Love without understanding *firstly* His Mercy, Goodness and Grace. God's *Mercy* is not getting what we do deserve. His *Goodness* reflects all of His dealings towards us which are pleasant. His *Grace* is getting what we don't deserve. But His Love is a combination of all of these and more. Now that we have had a thorough look at these three essential characteristics, we now have a foundation to correctly look at arguably His greatest attribute.

The word 'love' is an ambiguous word today. It is used for everything in our English language. We *love* our food, we *love* our favourite TV shows and sitcoms. We *love* cars, sporting teams, power and presents. And we sometimes *love* our family and friends. The world believes love is whatever makes us feel good and happy. Even if it means to use people in order to achieve this end. The deciding factor of love is ultimately this—selfishness centered or selflessness centered.

1 John 4 says, *This is love: not that we loved God, but that He loved us and sent His Son as an atoning sacrifice for our sins.* Let the magnitude of these words penetrate your every being. *This* is the definition of Love. God sending His Son to die on a cruel cross for a sinful humanity, taking their place of punishment and judgement. If most people can memorise John 3:16, we must also memorise 1 John 4:10. According to God—when a person is willing to serve another, lay down their life for them and even die for them, *that* is what true Love is. A Love totally unconditional, totally unselfish, and totally self-giving—perfectly expressed greatest on the Cross of Calvary.

The Love of God is a mystery in every way, transcending all understanding of human wisdom, rationale and thinking. Scripture clearly speaks of God's most striking manifestation of His love, not with gifts and presents, but by the death of Christ on a cross. God has exhibited His Greatness with the death of His only Son in our place of punishment. God's Love is expressed best by giving mankind a second chance to be redeemed from eternal wrath.

God's Love triumphs over all wickedness, overlooking a person's past and instead looking at the individual's potential good. Apart from God, we can not even begin to appreciate or understand what true Love is. When we truly know God and His Love, we can really love others as He loves us.

For God to acknowledge He is love is to admit that He is warm, friendly, affectionate and desires intimacy and relationship. It is a strange but beautiful idea. That God is free to share His identity, to be emotionally identified with fallen man. Furthermore, despite being all sufficient, He desires our love and will not be satisfied until He gets it.
—AW Tozer, pastor and author (1897-1963)[2]

In all honesty, there is absolutely no reason why a perfect, good and Holy God should love us. We knowingly disobey His commands and ways almost every day. There is no rational reason God loves us; He loves us, just because He does and chooses too. Psalm 136 is dedicated to this such truth, repeating '*His faithful love endures forever*'—twenty six times!

Christ died for sinners who were guilty and hateful; such that their everlasting destruction would be to the glory of God's justice. However, in His mercy Christ died to save us, from this eternal terror. While our character and condition loved our sin, committed it daily, and were slaves to it; with many being the chief and vilest of sinners; these were the ones Christ willingly died for. [3]

An Extraordinary Love

On his way to work one day, a Somali scholar, an expert in the Qur'an, was approached by an 11 year old Christian girl who told him, "Jesus loves you". Day after day, she stopped him with these same words. He first became annoyed, then downright angry until one morning her words changed. "I'd like to become a Muslim" she said, much to his delight!

But there was a catch. "I'll become a Muslim under one condition," she said, "that you show me in the Qur'an where it says Allah loves me". The scholar searched and searched, but nowhere in the Muslim holy book could he find those simple words. It was an omission that stirred his mind and haunted his heart. And that's when the miracle happened. He had a vision. He saw a cross floating in front of his eyes. He ran to the nearest Christian church where the pastor was a trained Bible League International worker.

The pastor explained God's plan of salvation, and that day he accepted Jesus Christ as his Saviour and received his first Bible. But the story does not end there. He too was discipled and trained by Bible League and is now leading his own Bible studies for Muslim seekers. "It's so important to me," shares this former Muslim, "to have Bibles and study materials, so that I can show them directly from the Scriptures the truth that a little child once shared with me. That God loves them". [4]

> *Now it is an extraordinary thing for one to give his life even for an upright man, though perhaps for a noble and lovable and generous benefactor someone might even dare to die. But <u>God shows and clearly proves His [own] love for us</u> by the fact that <u>while we were still sinners, Christ died for us.</u>*
> —Romans 5:7-8 AMP, author's emphasis

To God, the greatest illustration of love is shown when a life is given to save the life of another. This is especially so when the innocent takes the place of the wicked. While we were yet sinners and enemies, being dead in sin, committed it daily and slaves to it, with many the vilest of sinners, these were the ones Christ died for. In this His Love surpasses all that will ever been known to humanity.

Christ died for us in our place to save us from punishment. He took our place and by dying Himself on the Cross, He saved us from the greatest tragedy any person could ever experience—being separated from the Author of life.

> *Love is the only force capable of turning an enemy into a friend.*
> —Martin Luther King, American civil rights leader (1929-1968)

Though God created the heavens and the earth and all things belonged to Him, we were purchased at a great price. 1 Corinthians 6:19-20 says, *Do you not know that your body is the temple (the very sanctuary) of the Holy Spirit Who lives within you, Whom you have received [as a Gift] from God? You are not your own, you were bought with a price [purchased with a preciousness and paid for, made His own]. So then, honour God and bring glory to Him in your body.* Believers have been redeemed and recovered back to God. We were not bought with gold and silver, but with blood—the cost of a human life. For only He could pay the price that was owed, so great was the debt. Being bought you do not belong to yourself anymore. Your life is to now live for Him in a way that honours and pleases Him.

The greatest evidence of God's love was undertaken while we were enemies. From being enemies we were changed to friends. It was commenced by God and its foundation was laid while we were still hostile to it. The fact that we are purchased by His blood and sanctified by it, renders us sacred in His eyes. There is great value on us proportionate to the worth of the price of our redemption. And it is a pledge that He will keep what has been so dearly bought. [5]

> *For <u>God loved the world so much</u> that <u>He gave his one and only Son</u>, so that everyone who believes in Him will not perish but have eternal life. God sent his Son into the world not to judge the world, but to save the world through Him.*
> —John 3:16-17 NLT, author's emphasis

God has *proven* His Love in front of all the world. He has *demonstrated* His Love with the highest price in the universe. He has *confirmed* His Love and His *intention* in its purpose from the beginning. For the world to respond to His Love and be restored back into relationship. For all people from all tribes, communities, cities and nations to turn from wickedness and live in righteousness.

His Love is not like human love. We did not show Him any love, nor did we deserve it from any good works of ours. It was only because of His Sovereign will and pleasure. He designed to deliver us from sin and to work a great change in us. To be dead to sin and alive to Christ (Romans 6:11)! For God to love the sinner, the sinner to despise and hate the God, and for that God to die for them . . . is truly one of the greatest of all mysteries. For a righteous man to die in place of the unrighteous for no other reason but out of God's Sovereign Will and Love? We will have all of eternity to adore and wonder at its mystery for us individually . . .

The Nature of God is to Show Love

We know how much God loves us, and we have put our trust in his love. <u>God is love</u>, and all who live in love live in God, and God lives in them. And as we live in God, our love grows more perfect. So we will not be afraid on the Day of Judgement, but we can face him with confidence because we live like Jesus here in this world.
—1 John 4:16-17 NIV, author's emphasis

In the Greek, there are a number of words with distinct meanings translated by the one English word for 'love': 1) *agapê*—God's unconditional love, 2) *philia*—Friendship love, 3) *storgê*—Natural affection, 4) *eros*—Sexual love. The Greek word agapê, in particular when translated into English, is used as a term heavily charged with positive values: unconditional love, selfless love, *true* love—in any and every way that is good and wonderful, expressed towards others. Specifically, agapê love is used:

1) To express the essential nature of God (1 John 4:8);
2) His will to us concerning our behaviour towards other believers and toward all men (1 Thessalonians 3:12);
3) To describe the attitude of God toward His Son, the human race and to believe in Jesus Christ (see John 17:26; 3:16 and 14:21).

In my early days just recently saved, one of the most memorable revelations I had was simply that God loves me and accepts me just as I am. That His Love for me is not based on my performance or popularity, my personality or potential. His Love is not based on my faithfulness or my ability to be obedient or perfect in life. It is the fact that He loves me completely and unconditionally. How I can do nothing for Him to love me more, and nothing for Him to love me less. I can be no more righteous before Him now than any other time because of Christ's work on the cross. What's more, the fact that He sees the depth of my heart, all its flaws and sin and loves me the same. Now that is love!

A few years ago God put it on my heart to visit my grandma and buy her a brand new woman's devotional Bible. I drove over and helped out with moving belongings and some gardening. Later we sat down to talk and I showed her the Bible I bought her. She was surprised and said she has many Bibles (though I knew she didn't read them or attended church). I showed her the special features of it and eventually ended at 2 Corinthians 5:17-20:

> *Therefore, if anyone is in Christ, he is a new creation; the old has gone, the new has come! All this is from God, who reconciled us to himself through Christ and gave us the ministry of reconciliation: that God was reconciling the world to himself in Christ, not counting men's sins against them. And he has committed to us the message of reconciliation. We are therefore Christ's ambassadors, as though God were making his appeal through us. We implore you on Christ's behalf: Be reconciled to God.*

I explained the gospel and asked where she was at with God. She was not interested and became defensive. We argued about differences and meaningless topics. Upon leaving and walking to the car I challenged her with a final question: '*What if there was a God out there and He loved you? If there really was a God out there, somewhere, and He loved you. Wouldn't that change everything?*' That is the ultimate question everyone should ask themselves. People are relational and intimate beings. We desire and need affirmation, acceptance and approval. Just like the Muslim scholar who was sincere in his belief but was haunted at the idea that nowhere in the Qur'an did it say these simple words.

One of the most common questions I hear is *'If God is love why do bad things happen?'* This is a fair but narrow minded question. We often forget that *we* are the ones who make bad choices and then blame Him when everything falls apart. We are the ones who choose to live our own lives and God will continue to allow us to reap our consequences until we step back and allow Him to fix them. God does not cause wars, conflicts and commit crimes—we do. And with our own free-will, *we* choose to live how we desire, which is usually selfishly motivated at the expense of others. Proverbs 19:3 says *A man's own folly ruins his life, yet his heart rages against the LORD.*

God in His Love will never step over our free will. We are ultimately responsible for our decisions and all consequences that come with it. Theologians argue that the evidence of a Judgement Day is proved by the simple fact of our conscience. All people are instinctively born with the knowledge of good vs. evil and are given free will to choose for themselves. God will settle all accounts with both the righteous and unrighteous, according to all that they have done in their lifetime. 2 Corinthians 5:10 says *For we must all appear before the judgement seat of Christ, that each one may receive what is due him for the things done while in the body, whether good or bad.*

God's Great Love for His People

> *[Be] rooted and grounded in love, [so that you] may be able to comprehend with all the saints what is <u>the width and length and depth and height</u>—[which is] to know the love of Christ which passes knowledge . . .*
> *—Ephesians 3:17-19 AMP, author's emphasis*

When Paul wrote to the Ephesian church, he desired to express in the strongest sense of the greatness of the Love of God in the most emphatic manner possible. He wished that his readers would stop and meditate on this great and marvelous wonder, which comprehends all that is above, below, the past and the future. Let's take a look at this in better detail:

1) Breadth—all over the world
2) Length—to all people with the eternal message of the Gospel of Christ
3) Depth—reaches to the lowest fallen people
4) Height—reaches to the infinite heights to the throne of Christ

God's agapê love indicates that it is unconditional, selfless, sacrificial, extravagant, all comprehensive, 'your needs at my expense' approach. It also explains many of life's questions, including:

1) Why God creates—because He created people to love Him
2) Why God cares—we are made in His image and we need His help
3) Why we have free will—God wants a loving response from us, to accept/reject His love
4) Why Christ died—God's love caused Him to offer a solution to the problem of sin which separated us from His Love
5) Why there is Eternal life—God's love fully expresses itself to us forever, it never ends!

Scripture tells us we are to be firmly planted and established in our understanding of God's Love. Our trust in God must be founded in His Love for us. A foundation is what anything permanently rests upon and depends on for stability. God does not promise us an easy life without challenges, storms and trials. When Jesus came to earth and entered ministry, He was persecuted, accused of evil, slandered and betrayed. Finally, He was sentenced to a crime He didn't commit by a corrupted court of law and sentenced to the worst possible means of death. I say to many upcoming leaders under me when they start whining and complaining: '*You're not going to get it any better than Jesus. He didn't complain on the Cross!*'

What amazes me is Jesus never once thought twice that His Heavenly Father didn't Love Him when His circumstances showed otherwise. His foundation was completely rooted and grounded in the Fathers Love for Him, He trusted Him till the very end. Likewise, our foundation is to know God's outrageous Love for us, even when God doesn't make sense. To trust in His timing and plans because He Loves us completely. Even when I'm really hurting, my world is falling apart and

I want to walk away—I TRUST HIM because I know that I know that He Loves me. That God is for me and not against me. And all things work together for good, to those who love God and are called according to His purposes (Romans 8:28)!

Sadly, I have seen too many Christians walk away from God because they lost this amazing revelation. They let the storms of life, offences and misunderstandings shipwreck their faith. However, the truth is this should never happen. Once you know God's Love for you, it becomes your identity. When you know your Creator, you will know yourself, your purpose in life, calling and destiny. Outside of this relationship, there is no purpose. Nothing can satisfy or bring meaning and fulfillment.

I sometimes hear people casually saying after a preach at church, 'Yeah, yeah, I know God loves me'. They brush it over as if it is an elementary understanding and they are somehow more advanced. However, this should never be the case. God's Love does not end as a basic elementary truth from Sunday school. It is a *lifetime pursuit revelation* that we are to fully reflect and meditate on year after year, decade after decade. What else does God have to do to prove to you that He Loves you unconditionally, irrespective of your weaknesses and mistakes? That He Loves you completely, despite knowing all the good in you, all the bad in you, and all the ugly. And that His Love for us is greater than our understanding is to fully grasp it! All eternity we will marvel at this outrageous Love.

Our Response to this Great Love

And behold, a certain lawyer stood up and tested Him, saying, "Teacher, what shall I do to inherit eternal life?" He said to him, "What is written in the law? What is your reading of it?" So he answered and said, "You shall love the LORD your God with all your heart, with all your soul, with all your strength, and with all your mind,' and 'your neighbour as yourself.'" And He said to him, "You have answered rightly; do this and you will live."

—Luke 10:25-28 NKJV, author's emphasis

What do you say to a God that died for you? Our response is to *love the LORD your God with all your heart, with all your soul, with all your strength, and with all your mind.* With everything you are and with all of your being. Additionally, we are to love one another with the same affection. To the measure that you love people is the measure you love God. The law of love is to be written on our hearts for all to see. Without partiality or favourtism. Being religious does not excuse us from common courtesies and acts of kindness. When we love sacrificially and willingly, even when that love is not acknowledged, we are displaying the agapê love of God within us.

While serving at church one week, I was asked to call from a list of forty names to invite to our churches Christian Essentials course; a six week teaching on the foundations of the faith. Half way through the list I called a man named Tama. I was totally unprepared for what was to transpire in the next six hours. Just half an hour before I called he was praying in a church for a miracle. He was at the time homeless and living off the streets in the city of Sydney, unemployed and broke. To make matters worse he was from New Zealand and had lost all form of identification. No one would take him in for work or permanent housing. He had come to the end of himself and had lost all hope. And then I called.

He told me his story briefly and my heart went out to him. I advised him there was a church prayer meeting that night and he was welcome to come along. I negotiated to meet him half way and would drive him and his homeless buddy to church and promised to ask around to see if we could help him out. So, a few hours later, together with a friend of mine, I met Tama and his buddy and drove to church. If my mum had ever known she would have killed me (sorry mum!)

On arrival I spoke to the pastors and asked for their advice. It just so happened that a worker for the Salvation Army in the city was there that night who I had done Bible College with. He had connections with emergency shelter in the city and with one phone call they had two beds reserved by a tight deadline. No sooner had we arrived we had to leave. Tama mentioned he was hungry and hadn't eaten in two days. I stopped at a drive-thru McDonald's on the way and paid for all of us. We talked, we laughed and ate nasty junk food together. I dropped them off at the designated location, shook hands warmly and said goodbye. Half a tank of petrol later, I arrived home late at night, exhausted but fulfilled. I had shown sacrificial love to a complete stranger in a time of need he will never forget.

Paul gives a list of examples of just how this love is best reflected in everyday lives: *Love is patient, love is kind. It does not envy, it does not boast, it is not proud. It does not dishonour others, it is not self-seeking, it is not easily angered, it keeps no record of wrongs. Love does not delight in evil but rejoices with the truth. It always protects, always trusts, always hopes, always perseveres. Love never fails . . . And now these three remain: faith, hope and love. But the greatest of these is love* (1 Corinthians 13:4-8; 13 author's emphasis). Our response is to love one another with God's Love. Here we see a checklist for how you measure up to loving one another. There are opportunities to love someone sacrificially every day, but none more so than when it is leased deserved and unexpectant. This is what can turn a great enemy into a great friend. When Christians love people like this the world will come running to church to experience God's Love for themselves.

> *A new commandment I give to you, that you love one another; as I have loved you, that you also love one another. By this all will know that you are My disciples, if you have love for one another.*
> —John 13:35 NKJV, author's emphasis

Jesus Himself commanded us to love, which He says is the greatest proof that all people will know that we are His disciples. We are to live like Christ and live out His example to all people, great and small. The world will see Jesus when Christians love one another. When we forgive one another, serve, bless, and lay down our lives sacrificially. *Greater love has none other than this, that one lays down his life for his friend* (John 15:13). Jesus could not ask us to do something He Himself has not done already for us . . .

A Word of Warning

> *If someone says, "I love God," but hates a Christian brother or sister, that person is a liar; for if we don't love people we can see, how can we love God, whom we can*

not see? And he has given us this command: <u>Those who love God must also love their</u>
<u>*Christian brothers and sisters*</u>
—1 John 4:20-21 NIV, author's emphasis

Scripture clearly states that for a believer to confess they love God and pledge their allegiance to Him, but to not love another Christian, no matter what the circumstances, is to be a liar. They have denied their faith and are deceived of their true condition. It is a simple argument: if we refuse to love people we can see, how can we love God who we can not see? They are no different from the world and the wicked, who go through life loving, hating, envying and will be brought to nothing (Ecclesiastes 11:6).

I believe the world will see God when Christians love each other. The world will see Jesus when believers live in unity, peace and goodwill. When they lay down their lives for one another, forgive when offended, bless when cursed, serve when exhausted, and give when broke. There is no greater hypocrisy than when a people group claiming devotion to a faith act contrary to the faith altogether. We show ourselves to be most like God when we love the unlovable and those who belong in the family of God.

United we stand, divided we fall.
—Aesop, Greek writer (c.620-560BC)

Paul warns that in the last days, believers will lose the agapê love of God and be lovers of themselves, being deceived and deceiving others. *But mark this: There will be terrible times in the last days. People will be lovers of themselves, lovers of money, boastful, proud, abusive, disobedient to their parents, ungrateful, unholy, without love, unforgiving, slanderous, without self-control, brutal, not lovers of the good, treacherous, rash, conceited, lovers of pleasure rather than lovers of God—having a form of godliness but denying its power. Have nothing to do with them* (2 Timothy 3:1-5).

1 John 4:7-8 says, *Let us love one another, for love comes from God. Everyone who loves has been born of God and knows God. Whoever does not love does not know God, because God is love.* To love one another with God's unconditional agapê love is the

ultimate deciding factor of a Christian. This is to know God who is the author of Love itself. This is the strongest place a believer can ever be. Paul warned Timothy that in the last days, many professing Christians will lose the Love of God and fall away (see 2 Timothy 3:1-5).

Jude encourages us saying, *But you, beloved, building yourselves up on your most holy faith, praying in the Holy Spirit, keep yourselves in the love of God, looking for the mercy of our Lord Jesus Christ unto eternal life* (20-21, author's emphasis). When we keep ourselves in the love of God, we have guarded our hearts like a fortress and are standing firm in the truth, not swayed by people or circumstances. We will have nothing to worry about.

Love's Contemporary: God's Wrath

> *For the wrath of God is revealed from heaven against all ungodliness and unrighteousness of men, who suppress the truth in unrighteousness.*
> —Romans 1:18 NIV

This now brings us to an especially difficult but necessary truth. God's Love is wonderful and amazing, but for those who disregard it and treat it as common, they will never know it. The wrath of God is firstly His righteous anger at sin, expressed in Judgement. God is Holy and in His Holiness He must deal with it accordingly. Those who refuse to believe, repent, come to God and turn from wickedness God's wrath remains on them. God's righteousness requires His judgement upon sin. This does not reduce His love but on the contrary *supports* and *justifies* His love.

Consider this: Society has placed policeman and judges to deal with all types of crime within communities. We admire those who are opposed to evil and bring forth justice and punishment in order to promote peace and goodwill. Why shall we be not equally pleased with God, who is opposed to all sin which is a crime under the laws of the universe? Being Judge of the universe, He decides the proper timing and the appropriate punishment in order to preserve order and promote eternal peace.

But because of your <u>stubbornness</u> and <u>unrepentant heart</u> you are <u>storing up wrath for</u>
<u>yourself in the day of wrath</u> and revelation of the righteous judgement of God.
—Romans 2:5 NIV, author's emphasis

God's Mercy, Goodness, Grace and Love will not be abused forever. A day of reckoning will come. Those who have stubborn and unrepentant hearts are storing up for themselves God's wrath. Heaven keeps records and nothing is missed. Specifically God's wrath takes various forms and is separated into two categories:

a) The Present Wrath of God on earth for all to see—curses, tragedies, natural disasters, deaths etc. (Romans 1:18);

b) The Coming Wrath of God of Eternal Judgement—hell, a temporary holding area before Judgement Day (Luke 16:19-31) and then the Lake of Fire after Judgement Day (Revelation 20:15).

Ultimately all sin requires personal responsibility and ultimately separation from God. Sin is failure to live up to God's commands and always brings judgement. Sin should not be seen as a reward or enjoyment but a curse. *It is a terrible thing to fall into the hands of the living God* (Hebrews 10:31). People who have chosen to reject God and His offer of love and forgiveness have made the greatest mistake of their life. Scripture tells us that they are storing for themselves God's present and eternal wrath which will never ever end. They will have all of eternity to think about their decision.

"But when the Son of Man comes in his glory, and all the angels with him, then he
will sit upon his glorious throne. All the nations will be gathered in his presence, and
he will separate the people as a shepherd separates the sheep from the goats. He will
place the sheep at his right hand and the goats at his left . . ." Then the King will
turn to those on the left and say, 'Away with you, you cursed ones, into the eternal
<u>fire prepared for the devil and his demons</u> . . . <u>And they will go away into eternal</u>
<u>punishment</u>, but the righteous will go into eternal life."
—Matthew 25:31-33; 41; 46 NIV, author's emphasis

One of Paul's motivations for preaching the gospel was because *knowing the fear of the Lord we persuade men* (2 Corinthians 5:11). He knew just how much all mankind need the salvation of the gospel, because no one can escape God's wrath or enter heaven by their own works. Jesus is the only way we can be saved. For your soul to be saved and to enter heaven is everything. This can not be under-emphasised. Everything you were created for was to be in relationship with the Father. To be separated from that relationship is to literally lose everything you were created for. To miss heaven is the greatest tragedy man can ever know.

Example—Sodom and Gomorrah

Now this was the sin of your sister Sodom: she and her daughters were <u>arrogant, overfed and unconcerned;</u> they did not help the poor and needy. They were haughty and did detestable things before Me. Therefore I did away with them . . .
—Ezekiel 16:49-50 NIV, author's emphasis

Sodom and Gomorrah were two cities in Abraham's day that were known to be unusually wicked. The people had reduced themselves to absurd idolatries and degraded themselves by the most abominable deeds. Theologians record that they had reduced themselves to sexual relations between parents and children, demon worship, baby sacrifices to false gods and even sex with animals. Society had reached a point of total depravity with no return. Below is a fascinating except from an article presenting a genuine theory of how Sodom and Gomorrah were destroyed:

The ruins of Sodom and Gomorrah have been discovered southeast of the Dead Sea. The modern names are Bab edh-Dhra, thought to be Sodom, and Numeira, thought to be Gomorrah. Both places were destroyed at the same time by an enormous inferno of some type. The destruction debris was about three feet thick. Startling discoveries in the cemetery at Bab edh-Dhra revealed that buildings used to bury the dead were burned by a fire that started on the roof.

The cities might have been destroyed as the result of a natural cataclysm. It is possible that the towns were destroyed by an earthquake in the region, especially if the towns laid along a major fault line. What would cause every structure in the cemetery to be destroyed in this way? The only conceivable explanation for this unique discovery in the annals of archaeology is that burning debris fell on the buildings from the air.

There is ample evidence of subterranean deposits of a petroleum-based substance called bitumen, similar to asphalt, in the region south of the Dead Sea. Such material normally contains a high percentage of sulfur. It has been postulated by geologist Frederick Clapp that pressure from an earthquake could have caused the bitumen deposits to be forced out of the earth through a fault line. As it gushed out of the earth it could have been ignited by a spark or surface fire. It would then fall to earth as a burning, fiery mass.

It was only after Clapp formulated this theory that Sodom and Gomorrah were found. It turns out that the sites are located exactly on a fault line along the eastern side of a plain south of the Dead Sea. Clapp's theory is entirely plausible. [6]

Genesis 19:24; 28 says, *Then the LORD <u>rained down burning sulfur on Sodom and Gomorrah</u>—from the LORD out of the heavens. Thus He overthrew those cities and the entire plain, destroying all those living in the cities—and also the vegetation in the land . . . Abraham looked down toward Sodom and Gomorrah, toward all the land of the plain, and he saw dense smoke rising from the land, <u>like smoke from a furnace</u>* (author's emphasis). The destruction of Sodom and Gomorrah became an example in the Bible of how God judges and deals with sin.

Hell was never more visible on earth than when Sodom and Gomorrah were fully ablaze. God's wrath is His final action. He takes no pleasure in the destruction of the wicked, but must execute justice which He rules His Kingdom in righteousness. Our response to Him determines His response to us. Make no mistake: God's Love is certain, but so is His Wrath.

Final Thoughts

God's Love is the theme of the Bible—from Genesis to Revelation. Hebrews 13:8 declares *He is the same yesterday, today and forever.* We can therefore trust that His love is constant and eternal. That it never changes, never stops, and never runs out. That it is always available every day, unconditionally. Let heaven and earth stand amazed at His love which lasts forever.

And I am convinced that nothing can ever separate us from God's love. Neither death nor life, neither angels nor demons, neither our fears for today nor our worries about tomorrow—not even the powers of hell can separate us from God's love. No power in the sky above or in the earth below—indeed, nothing in all creation will ever be able to separate us from the love of God that is revealed in Christ Jesus our Lord
—Romans 8:38-39 NLT

To those who respond and choose God have nothing to worry about. You were made for His Love. You were created to be extravagantly Loved. To be affectionately Loved by Him alone. His Love for you makes you valuable, precious and worthy, regardless of anything you do, good or bad. This is the Love of God for you! Certainly, if there is Amazing Grace, this is Amazing Love.

CHAPTER 7

The Peace of God

Jesus proclaimed peace and good-will to all men who choose Him.
He is the great Peacemaker; restoring our relationship with God once
separated and broken beyond repair.

*Now may the God of peace who brought up our Lord Jesus from the dead, that great
Shepherd of the sheep, through the blood of the everlasting covenant, make you complete
in every good work to do His will, working in you what is well pleasing in His sight,
through Jesus Christ, to whom be glory forever and ever. Amen.*
—Hebrews 13:20-21 NKJV, author's emphasis

*Long ago a rich man desired to find the perfect picture of peace. Being troubled with
constant worry from finances and relationships, he wanted a painting to gaze at when
his mind was in turmoil. He announced a contest throughout all the lands to produce
this masterpiece. The prize would be great. The challenge stirred the imagination of
artists everywhere, and thousands of paintings arrived from countries far and wide.*

*Finally the great day of the contest arrived. He uncovered one peaceful scene after
another, while a gathered audience clapped and cheered. After many viewings he was
still not satisfied. Only two pictures remained veiled. As he pulled the cover from one,
a hush fell over the crowd. A mirror-smooth lake reflected lacy, green birches under the
soft blush of the evening sky. Along the grassy shore, a flock of sheep grazed undisturbed.
Could this be peace?*

*The man uncovered the second painting and the crowd gasped in surprise. A tumultuous
waterfall cascaded down a rocky precipice. Stormy gray clouds threatened to explode*

143

with lightning, wind and rain. But in the midst of the thundering noises and bitter chill, a spindly tree clung to the rocks at the edge of the falls. A little sparrow had built her nest in the depths of the branch. Content and undisturbed in her stormy surroundings, she rested on her eggs. With her eyes closed and her wings covering her little ones, she manifested peace that transcended all human understanding . . .[1]

In a world fuelled by fear, violence and evil, we can easily go through life with anything but peace. A former president of the Norwegian Academy of Sciences and historians from England, Egypt, Germany, and India came up with some startling information. Since 3,600 B.C. the world has known only 292 years of peace! During this period there have been:

- 14,351 wars, large and small;
- 3.64 billion people directly or indirectly killed;
- The value of the property destroyed would pay for a golden belt around the world 97.2 miles wide and 33 feet thick;
- Since 650 B.C. there have been 1,656 arms races, with only 16 of which have not ended in war, the remainder ended in economic collapse.[2]

Billions of dollars are spent every year on therapists, psychologists and medical treatment. All some people have ever known is anxiety, depression and fear. General practioners today are visited by some 50 percent of their patients for depression related sicknesses. Disappointment and despair is tearing apart relationships, leading to record highs of stress leave, depression and suicide. Not surprisingly society has never become more cynical and negative about so many un-important issues than ever before. But this does not have to be the case! When Christ went to the cross, He not only removed our sins and diseases but brought us Peace with God and each other. Before, there was separation and wrath, Christ brought us complete reconciliation, forgiveness and Peace. Horizontally to God and vertically to all men.

Peace is defined by Strong in the Greek as *eirene*, being *a state of rest, calmness, absence of strife, and harmonious relationships between God and men, man to man.*[3] It is to have a peace of conscience knowing ones sins are forgiven when asked for it, peace at all times and in all circumstances. Hebrews 13 says, *Now may the God of peace . . . make you complete in every good work to do His will, working in you what is well pleasing in His sight.* We serve the God of Peace. He takes away every stress, anxiety and fear known to man. When the world is falling apart, you have lost hope and you've come to the end of yourself, we are to go to the God of Peace. Only He can calm our storms and restore our minds to perfect Peace.

> *For the kingdom of God is not a matter of eating and drinking, but of righteousness, peace and joy in the Holy Spirit, because anyone who serves Christ in this way is pleasing to God and approved by men.*
> —Romans 14:17-18 NIV, author's emphasis

Scripture says heaven is a place of complete righteousness, peace and joy in the Holy Spirit. The Kingdom is a city of total peace, unity and harmony in every way. Its citizens are to live and spread this peace in a world of chaos, fear and confusion. This is what pleases God and makes us approved by man. The key to this treasure is relationship in Christ. Romans 5:1-2 says, *. . . since we have been justified through faith, we have peace with God through our Lord Jesus Christ, through whom we have gained access by faith into this grace in which we now stand* (author's emphasis). The greatest need for humanity is for all people to have peace with God. To be justified through faith in Christ. Only when cities and nations look to God will all wars cease and the world will know true peace.

Philippians 4:7 says *The peace of God, which transcends all understanding, will guard your hearts and your minds in Christ Jesus.* God's peace is not of this world—it resides only in the hearts of believers in Christ. Christ keeps us in Peace wherever He dwells and rules. It is a mystery and beyond words. It transcends all human understanding and thinking. His Peace is unknowable, unsearchable. It has the power to guard our hearts and minds in the midst of adversity. The word 'guard' is a military term meaning to guard our hearts like a castle. The heart is the seat of all our affections and passions which control all areas of our life. If it is not guarded carefully we are at risk of falling very easily. But with this Peace we are protected from the worst enemies to the human soul—fear, anxiety and worry.

> *Lord, make me a channel of your peace.*
> —St Francis of Assisi, Italian Catholic Friar (c. 1181-1226)

The Peace of God is essential in life because our mind and heart have the power to control every area of our life. Put simply: *Thoughts* affect *emotions*, which impact our *attitudes*, then create *actions* leading to *habits*. Over time our habits become our *lifestyle* and will turn into our *destiny*. All of this begins with our thoughts. It is estimated that we think approximately 70,000 thoughts per day. If even half of these are negative, angry or self-critical, we will live very difficult lives! You are the sum total of your thoughts right now which is why it is so important to guard them so carefully. In Christ we will have the power to guard them against anything that will hinder us.

Blessed are the Peacemakers

> *Blessed (enjoying enviable happiness, spiritually prosperous—with life-joy and satisfaction in God's favour and salvation, regardless of their outward conditions) <u>are the makers and maintainers of peace</u>, for they shall be called the sons of God!*
> —Matthew 5:9 AMP author's emphasis

For peacemakers to get a place in the eight beatitudes is remarkable. Life is amazing when relationships are amazing. There is nothing greater in life than all of our relationships being at peace and full of harmony. But this is not always guaranteed. As an ambassador of Christ, we are to be God's peacemakers in this world as conflict divides families and nations. God moves in unity and peaceful relationships.

Psalm 133:1 says something amazing: *Where there is unity God commands a blessing.* God takes great joy and happiness when His people are unified and at peace with one another. It is significant that when Pentecost arrived, the Holy Spirit came when all the apostles and believers were in agreement with one heart, one mind, one vision and one purpose. *When the day of Pentecost was fully come, they were all with one accord in one place* (Acts 2:1, author's emphasis). God can not move in souls who are divided, divisive and in discord.

Now, let us not confuse a *peacemaker* with a *peacekeeper*. A peacekeeper avoids confrontation and sweeps everything under the carpet pretending nothing is wrong. They will say outwardly that everything is fine, but deep down there is bitterness and conflict. This is 'superficial peace' which does not last and will soon be exposed. On the other hand, a peacemaker will go in love and confront the conflict in the hope of positive reconciliation. They desire openness, truth and love, bringing everything hidden to the surface. Here the relationship is what matters and not necessarily the result. These are the ones Jesus calls 'sons of God', as they imitate His likeness. God is a God of relationship and community. To Him all relationships are everything and are worth fighting for. Peacemakers must be bold and courageous, fighting battles which sometimes aren't their own. All to ensure peace rules and reigns at the end of the day.

I am not suggesting that a person living in total peace has to be a monk living in the mountains, going out of their way to avoid environments of conflict. A peacemaker takes the hard road. In times of chaos and even times of warfare among the closest family and friends, they are there actively bringing reconciliation and peace.

Peacemakers are to love and delight in peace. They keep the peace when it is not broken, and recover it when it is not present. A true peacemaker is guided and motivated by the Good News that God has made peace with us through Christ. They no longer live in conflict or attacking others for personal gain or selfish ambitions. They desire peace between themselves and God, and towards all people. [4]

Heaven is a place of Peace because God is Peace. He loves peaceful relationships and unity among His people and hates it when there it division, distrust and discord. 1 Corinthians 14:33 says, *For God is not a God of disorder but of peace, as in all the meetings of God's holy people.* We are never more like God than when we are imitating Him, bringing peace to situations, especially in the most difficult of circumstances. Peacemakers are expected to promote reconciliation and unity at all times and in all areas, without prejudice.

If the peacemakers are blessed, it must be a given that the peace breakers are cursed. The bible is full of warnings against the practices of those who bring division and disunity amongst relationships. These are the characteristics of the devil, who knows the power of strong relationships in church, leadership and marriages. Of the seven practices and sins God detests, the *one who sows discord among brethren* is an abomination (see Proverbs 6:16-19). They will not go unpunished.

Christ is the Great Prince of Peace

> *For to us a child is born, to us a son is given, and the government will be on his shoulders. And he will be called Wonderful Counselor, Mighty God, Everlasting Father, Prince of Peace. Of the Greatness of His government and peace there will be no end.*
>
> —Isaiah 9:6-7 NIV, author's emphasis

When Isaiah wrote these words he saw a glimpse of a great and glorious event. During times of great evil and darkness, he saw a light rising in the distant. This man would end all wars and His titles would show His power and authority. His Greatness rules His government in Peace. A Kingdom that will never end. Jesus is the Prince of Peace. The One who mediates a perfect God with a fallen mankind. No man can make his own peace with God except on His terms. He is the Way, the Truth and the Light to a relationship with God (John 14:6).

His government will be righteously administered and will be ruled with Peace lasting forever. Upon His shoulders He will rule with an iron scepter, dashing His enemies and protecting those under His care. These offices are one of the greatest honours and fit for only one who has the same character as God Himself—Jesus Christ. He will be called by His Titles:

1) **Wonderful Counselor**—He is wonderful in His person, that He should be God and man in one person, and have two natures. Wonderful in the disposition of His mind and in the qualities He possesses in His love to His people. Wonderful in His humility, meekness and patience. And wonderful in His wisdom, conduct and soul. [5]

2) **Mighty God**—the government shall be upon his shoulder, the world and the Heavens God granted Him, effectively the keys to the universe. He is King of all the saints; His government consists in ruling in the hearts of His people, supplying them with everything necessary and subduing His enemies.[6]

3) **Everlasting Father**—He is the completeness of the Father of knowledge, Father of goodness and Father of Peace, everlasting through all of Eternity.[7]

4) **Prince of Peace**—His royal proclamation is the gospel of peace, the fruit of His Spirit is peace and his subjects are peaceable ones. He is a Prince superior to kings, being the Prince of the kings of the earth. [8]

Peace I leave with you; my peace I give you. I do not give to you as the world gives.
Do not let your hearts be troubled and do not be afraid.
—John 14:27 NIV, author's emphasis

Before Jesus left earth He promised His disciples the one thing they would need most for the battles ahead. Jesus knew the many trials and adversities that would soon come against them, so He promised them His Peace. This is the greatest gift He could leave us with, next to the Holy Spirit. His Peace isn't sitting in an isolated temple with your legs crossed, your thumb touching your pinky and humming. It is permanent, real, genuine and authentic Peace from Heaven. Whatever the world offers is temporary and counterfeit.

Colossians 3:15 says, *Let the peace of Christ rule in your hearts, since as members of one body you were called to peace. And be thankful.* The Peace of God must be our umpire in life which rules and reigns in our hearts and minds. Can a body live in war with itself and still live? As believers, it is our mandate to live in love and peace—not an army divided and at war with itself. From this place we are to be always thankful. And there is much to be thankful for.

Rejoice in the Lord always [delight, gladden yourselves in Him]; again I say, Rejoice!
Let all men know and perceive and recognise your unselfishness (your considerateness,
your forbearing spirit). The Lord is near [He is coming soon]. <u>*Do not fret or have*</u>
<u>*any anxiety about anything, but in every circumstance and in everything, by*</u>
<u>*prayer and petition (definite requests), with thanksgiving,*</u> *continue to make your*
wants known to God. And God's peace [shall be yours, that tranquil state of a soul
assured of its salvation through Christ, and so fearing nothing from God and being
content with its earthly lot of whatever sort that is, that peace] which transcends all
understanding shall garrison and mount guard over your
hearts and minds in Christ Jesus.
—Philippians 4:4-7 AMP, author's emphasis

The Christian, committing his ways to God, has a peace which is nowhere else to be found. This peace keeps us from all anxiety, agitation and concerns, regardless of anything external. Peace is an internal issue of the heart and when guarded against external circumstances it can be a powerful force. Notice in Philippians 4 that it is given to us through a series of steps:

1) **Rejoice in the Lord**—taking delight in God, remembering that He loves you, has saved you and you are blessed with every spiritual blessing. Make God's Goodness your focus, not your problems and worries.

2) **Gentleness**—let all men know that you are unselfish and considerate in all you do, have a lifestyle and a spirit of gentleness follow you wherever you go.

3) **Do not be anxious**—choosing not to allow negative circumstances come into your heart and bring anxiety, fear and worry. We are not always in control of what is around us but we are always in control of how we respond to them.

4) **Prayer**—making our requests known to God, anything and everything, if it matters to you it matters to God. Have faith that He is bigger than our problems and nothing is impossible with Him.

5) **Petitions**—a formal request addressed to a person in authority in writing made to a court, requesting judicial action concerning some matter. It

is specific, detailed and time bound. Desperate times call for desperate measures. Guaranteed for fast results when done correctly.

6) **Thanksgivings**—being always thankful is paramount, we are to enter into His presence with thanksgiving and enter into His courts with praise (Psalm 100:4). There is so much to be thankful for to God, create a climate of thanksgiving and gratitude in your life everyday.

7) **Requests**—in faith, ask expectantly and boldly, speaking what is not into existence. Your words are powerful, there is power to pull down heavens resources if you simply believe. Stop looking at what you don't yet currently have, and focus instead on what you do have.

Humble yourselves, therefore, under God's mighty hand, that he may lift you up in due time. Cast all your anxiety on him because he cares for you.
—1 Peter 5:6-7 NIV, author's emphasis

We are promised that when we do these seven steps we will *then* receive the Peace of God. His Peace comes after *constant* prayer; not occasional sporadic prayer. This peace will keep us from sinning under troubles and from sinking under them. God does not enjoy seeing His children burdened with unnecessary anxieties and fears. When we cast our anxiety and troubles all onto Him, He promises to take them from us because He deeply cares for us.

The Peace of God was purchased by Christ on the cross for us to share and enjoy. It is made available through the power and influence of the Holy Spirit. We have peace because we have full assurance that our names are written in the Book of Life. Joy in God is of great reward which far outweighs all known sorrows. It is to be our constant pursuit and hearts delight.[9]

Our Response to the God of Peace

If it is possible, as far as it depends on you, live at peace with everyone.
—Romans 12:18 NIV author's emphasis

Our response to this peace is to live in peace with one another. Never in constant hostilities and jealousies. These are the weapons and strategies of the devil and how his kingdom operates. Romans 12 says, *if it is possible*, meaning it is just simply not possible to live in peace with everyone. This I can quickly testify too! We are all uniquely different and have many separate views, opinions and expectations of one another. No wonder relationships are so challenging! However, just because they are at times difficult does not mean we are excused to cut them off. Relationships are not optional—they are *essential*. All great relationships have a heart-to-heart connection which we need to fight for. We need each other more than we dare to admit because life was not meant to be lived alone.

It is the believer's duty to live peaceably where they dwell and pray for the peace of the place where they are. They should live peaceably with their very enemies, if it is possible, for there are some persons of such tempers and dispositions it is impossible to live peaceably with. For when others are for peace, they are for war. But as far as it depends on you. Nothing should be wanting on our part. Every step we take should be taken to cultivate and maintain peace.[10]

Before I came to Christ, my life was ruled by fear, worry and anxiety. To numb these emotions I became very angry and most of my relationships were full of conflict. I channelled this anger by playing violent computer games which I soon became addicted too, playing for days and weeks on end. LAN parties were often, where my mates and I would stay up all night eating junk food and digitally killing each other over and over again. Not surprisingly my life was not one I was proud of and many years were wasted. On the outside I was a nice person but on the inside my heart was full of violence, anger, bitterness and selfishness. I actually had the dream of joining the army when I finished school so I could own a machine gun and shoot people for real.

Years later, a Christian friend told me of a day in high school once. He remembered talking with all the other Christians about reaching out to me with God. They laughed at the idea and could never believe I would be interested and could be saved! I thought for a moment when I heard that, '*Thanks a lot!*' But that day I believe was a challenge to God that He could bring me to Himself and radically change my life. Only a year later a work colleague, who also got radically transformed from drug rehab in Coffs Harbour, was doing Bible College and invited me to *C3 Oxford Falls*. Three weeks later I was at the altar and rededicated my life to Christ. But it doesn't end there. Several months later I was on fire for God and a changed man. Later on, I remember observing the Christians who laughed that I could be saved, and telling them they were lukewarm and needed to repent! God definitely does have a sense of humour.

Now, when I first became saved I still struggled with the addiction of playing violent computer games. But God was Faithful. One thing that meant more to me than computer games was independence and driving a car. When the week approached for me to get my provisional driver's licence, I had absolutely no confidence in myself (it took me four attempts just to get my learners licence!) So I prayed, *Father, if you will help me get my licence first time, I promise to never play violent computer games ever again.'*

The day came and everything went smoothly. There was no traffic on the road and the test was a near 100% score. I got my provisional licence. Remembering my oath I gave away all my games and consoles which was not easy. Weeks and months went by and all I could think about was those games! I even had dreams about being the hero and killing everyone in the level! But slowly, through God's Grace, my mind was renewed and the desire for them ceased. I have kept my oath to God since, and furthermore, have never had even one car accident. Praise God!

Peace's Contemporary: Anxiety

> *My heart is in anguish within me; the terrors of death assail me.*
> *Fear and trembling have beset me; horror has overwhelmed me.*
> —Psalm 55:4-5 NIV

Anxiety can be caused by many reasons including lack of sleep, personal fears, a stressful work environment or an unsustainable lifestyle. Sometimes life just throws us daily challenges that keep us on our feet just like everybody else. Another word for fear is anxiety. Anxiety is the opposite of peace, just as fear and hate are the opposites of faith and love. Anxiety is a sign of the absence of trust in God which can come from many sources. It is a product of the flesh (an unsurrendered life) and not of the Spirit who lives within us (a truly surrendered life). Most importantly anxiety is not of faith and chooses not to trust God or acknowledge that He is in complete control. Anxiety is not good for us because *an anxious heart weighs a man down* (Proverbs 12:25).

Most of us worry unnecessarily about too many things. It is almost as though we search for problems to give ourselves stress. The amazing news is that much of what we worry about doesn't matter at all! Take a look at these statistics about worry:

- 40% of all things that we worry about never come to pass;
- 30% of all our worries involve past decisions that can not be changed;
- 12% focus on criticism from others who spoke because they felt inferior;
- 10% are related to our health, which gets worse when we worry;
- 8% of our worries could be described as 'legitimate' causes for concern.

How about that? Less than one worry in every ten that we worry about is a real concern. All the others are things that we can learn to see differently or eliminate altogether.[11] The world promises temporary peace when we pursue pleasure, fame, and wealth but leaves only emptiness and regret. Philosophy and false religions profess to give peace, but it is not real or lasting. It does not still the voice of conscience, take away the guilt of sin, or reconcile the soul to God.

There is nothing wrong with acknowledging serious problems in life. But it is wrong and unhealthy to be immobilised by excessive worry. Such worry must be committed to prayer to God, who can release us from paralyzing fear or anxiety, and free us to deal with the needs and welfare of others. Severe anxiety is known to lead to many health related issues such as high blood pressure, depression, panic attacks and anxiety disorders. Ultimately, anxiety is sin because it chooses not to trust in God and His ability to move in even impossible situations. It is to limit

God by putting Him in a box telling Him what is possible and what is not. God is never anxious, fearful or worried. Anxiety comes upon us when our focus is totally consumed on self and our inabilities. Pity the fool who lives a life dominated by never ending fears and anxieties of every kind.

Friend, if you're struggling with anxieties Christ desires to set you free. Your battle is with the Lord. What you believe is impossible is very possible with Him. He loves impossible circumstances. Turn to Him today, seek His guidance, let some things go and be everything He created you to be. In reality 99 percent of all anxiety, fears and worries today won't matter in twelve months' time. Have perspective of the bigger picture and an eternal mindset.

> *The beginning of anxiety is the end of faith and the*
> *beginning of true faith is the end of anxiety.*
> —George Müller, Prussian Evangelist and humanitarian (1805-1898)

Example—The Life of King Saul

> *When the men were returning home after David had killed [Goliath], the women*
> *came out from all the towns of Israel . . . singing and dancing . . . "Saul has slain*
> *his thousands, and David his tens of thousands." Saul was very angry; this refrain*
> *displeased him greatly. "They have credited David with tens of thousands," he*
> *thought, "but me with only thousands. What more can he get but the kingdom?"*
> *And from that time on Saul kept a close eye on David.*
> —1 Samuel 18:6-9 NIV

King Saul was chosen by God, anointed to be king, started with a win in battle, and loved by the people. But he had a tragic end. His life was fuelled by anxiety, worry and fear which fed his jealousies ultimately leading to his destruction. His life was ruled by his emotions and the threat to his throne, even though God Himself had given it to him in the first place. Instead of a king who served God's purposes, he became an evil tyrant. His anxieties made him make one bad decision after another, with complete disregard to the consequences to himself and others.

When David courageously defeated Goliath in battle and defeated the Philistines, the whole nation was in celebration. He was loved by the soldiers and women, with songs sung about him and his victories over Israel's enemies. However, Saul somehow saw this young, loyal shepherd boy as a threat. This is a typical response of a religious person. Our true nature is revealed when we see the success and favouritism of others. Instead of rejoicing with them, they are envious and spiteful. They forget all the wonderful blessings God has done for them and focus instead on the one thing someone else has just had victory over. They let someone else's success threaten them and are bound by the fear of man. Insecurity and low self-worth are a breeding ground for jealousies and hostilities. *For wherever there is jealousy and selfish ambition, there you will find disorder and evil of every kind* (James 3:16).

Saul's insecurities led him to be envious, suspicious, bitter and then murderous towards David. His anxieties and fears soon brought out the worst in him. Finally the presence of God left him and an evil spirit controlled his life. Soon he would be chasing David senselessly with three-thousand soldiers through the desert and mountains to hunt down this simple shepherd boy who simply had a heart after God. The prophet Samuel rebukes him for disobedience and prophecies the end of his rule:

> *But now your kingdom must end, for the LORD has sought out a man after his own heart. The LORD has already appointed him to be the leader of his people, because you have not kept the LORD's command.*
> —1 Samuel 13:14 NIV

However it didn't end there. Saul's anger led to rage and then to murder. A man with much power but no accountability leads to great evil. Upon hearing that the priests at Nob had helped David with food and weapons, Saul ordered that all eighty-five innocent priests and the whole town be killed. *The king then ordered Doeg, "You turn and strike down the priests." So Doeg the Edomite turned and struck them down. That day he killed eighty-five men who wore the linen ephod. He also put to the sword Nob, the town of the priests, with its men and women, its children and infants, and its cattle, donkeys and sheep* (1 Samuel 22:17-19). Saul's small anxieties and fears soon turned him into an evil tyrant and madman.

Though David was the most loyal, diligent and godly servant in Saul's army, he falsely believed that David was disloyal and his motives were to dethrone and take the kingdom himself. He is deceived and becomes his own worst enemy. Finally Saul is wounded in battle and ends his life committing suicide. He failed test after test. His life was characterised by selfishness, disobedience and lust for power. He had so much potential and yet failed so much. His legacy to us today is by refusing to let go of our anxieties into God's hands, they are certain to bring upon us great pain and sorrows.

Final Thoughts

Philippians 4:6-7 says, *Do not be anxious about anything, but in everything, by prayer and petition, with thanksgiving, present your requests to God, then the peace of God, which transcends all understanding, will guard your hearts and your minds in Christ Jesus.* Peace comes after constant prayer. In order to eliminate anxiety, Christ needs to rule and reign in our hearts. Jesus left His disciples more than just wishful thinking. It was a promise from the One who has power to make Peace for us and transfer it to all He desires to give it to.

> *Let us fix our eyes on Jesus, the author and perfecter of our faith, who for the joy set before him endured the cross, scorning its shame, and sat down at the right hand of the throne of God. Consider him who endured such opposition from sinful men, so that you will not grow weary and lose heart*
> —Hebrews 12:2-3 NIV

When our eyes are not fixed on Christ we are in danger of focusing all of our attention on the storms around us and allowing our hearts to be filled with much grief. But when we are living by the Spirit within us, we will display the fruits and results of the Spirit, a peace that surpasses all understanding.

CHAPTER 8

The Faithfulness of God

Because God is Faithful, everything He does is Good,
Perfect and Divine.

*God is faithful (reliable, trustworthy and therefore ever true to His promise,
and He can be depended on); by Him you were called into companionship
and participation with His Son, Jesus Christ our Lord.*
—1 Corinthians 1:9 AMP, author's emphasis

*S*enator Mark Hatfield told friends and family once of his time touring Calcutta,
India with Mother Teresa. He was visiting with her the so-called 'House of Dying',
where sick children are cared for in their last days, and the dispensary. The poorest of
the poor line up by the hundreds to receive urgent medical attention, often with a day
to live.

Watching Mother Teresa minister to these people, feeding and nursing those left by
others to die, Hatfield was overwhelmed by the sheer magnitude of the suffering she
and her co-workers faced daily. "How can you bear the load without being crushed by
it?" he asked.

Mother Teresa replied, "My dear Senator, I am not called to be successful, like you and
your culture thinks. I am called to be faithful . . ." [1]

This brings us to our next study—the Faithfulness of God. Though we change every day, He never changes through all eternity. If He is unchanging He can never be accused of being unfaithful since that would require Him to change. The Faithfulness of God is a favourite expression among the ancient Jews. By it they properly understand the integrity of God in preserving whatever is entrusted to Him. And out of all creation, He is above all Faithful to His people.

Faithfulness is defined by many as steadfast in affection or allegiance, devoted, and utterly trustworthy. 1 Corinthians 1:9 says, *God is faithful (reliable, trustworthy and therefore ever true to His promise, and He can be depended on); by Him you were called into companionship and participation with His Son, Jesus Christ our Lord.* Just as God is Love, He is Faithful. He is the definition of Faithfulness. Like a husband vows to be faithful to his wife, we are also called to be faithful to our Father in Heaven. We are to have no idols or contemporaries. God alone is to be our delight and focus. James 4:5 says, *Or do you think Scripture says without reason that the spirit he caused to live in us envies intensely?* He is jealous for our affection and loyalty.

> *Know therefore that the LORD your God is God; He is the faithful God, keeping his covenant of love to a thousand generations of those who love Him and keep His commands.*
> —Deuteronomy 7:9 NIV

In the Hebrew, faithfulness is translated as *emunah*, meaning *firmness, stability, steadiness, that which is permanent, enduring and steadfast.* [2] God is firm, stable and steadfast in His Faithfulness. He is unmovable and totally enduring in His Faithfulness towards us. Like a devoted husband is faithful to his wife till death, so are we to be faithful in our relationship with God. Deuteronomy 7:9 says He keeps His covenant of Love to a thousand generations. Written 3,000 years ago, God is *still* faithful today. He has proven His Faithfulness again and again, with every generation and every one to follow

Psalm 36:5 says *Your love, O LORD, reaches to the heavens, your faithfulness to the skies*. To paint a picture in our minds, the psalmist declares that God's Faithfulness reaches to the skies. Now, the distance from the ground to the earth's atmosphere is approximately over 100 kilometers. That's a pretty big distance! Furthermore, Psalm 89:5 says, *The Heavens praise your wonders LORD, your faithfulness too, in the assembly of the Holy Ones*. All of heavens millions of angels, princes, kings, and saints praise His wonders in the assembly of the trinity of the God-head. His Faithfulness is emphasised next to His wonders.

> *Instead of their shame my people will receive a double portion, and instead of disgrace they will rejoice in their inheritance; and so they will inherit a double portion in their land, and everlasting joy will be theirs. "For I, the LORD, love justice; I hate robbery and iniquity. In my faithfulness I will reward them and make an everlasting covenant with them.*
> —Isaiah 61:7-8 NIV, author's emphasis

Previously, Israel had been unfaithful and was exiled from the Promised Land. They had suffered the punishment of their sins and the sins for their fathers. They had experienced great shame and disgrace at the hands of the Babylonians. All the nations mocked that the God who freed them from Egyptian slavery and destroyed their enemies, had now turned on them and forgotten them. That they would never be the great nation they once were. But despite their unfaithfulness God promises His people a *double portion* of blessings and favour. He will look on them with mercy, deliver and save them, and restore their fortunes. They will enjoy the land again and experience everlasting joy. To guarantee this, God makes a covenant. In His Faithfulness He will reward them if they turn back to Him and turn from their evil ways.

His Faithfulness can be trusted and entirely relied upon. This account of Israel applies just as much for us today. If we have fallen away and been unfaithful, God desires to restore us with a double portion. He wants us to fully experience everlasting joy in His presence. This is the Faithfulness of God!

The Nature of God is to Show Faithfulness

If we are faithless [do not believe and are untrue to Him], He remains true (faithful to
His Word and His righteous character), for He can not deny Himself.
—2 Timothy 2:13 AMP, author's emphasis

Even if we are unfaithful He remains Faithful. Man becomes unfaithful out of desire, fear, and weakness, lack of character or a combination of all. But *God is Faithful*, even in the midst of our sin and failures. Even when we were a thousand miles away from God and lived in rebellion, He was still Faithful and loved us. Amazing!

2 Samuel 22:26-27 says, *To the faithful you show yourself faithful; to those with integrity you show integrity. To the pure you show yourself pure, but to the wicked you show yourself hostile.* How we live determines God's response to us. He repays us for our consistent behaviour—good or bad. Every individual is responsible for how they live. They are either faithful or unfaithful, to man and God. They are either integrous or wicked, to all people and Him. God is Faithful to His word for His word is His bond. Men say and promise one thing and do another. Their word is subject to change according to what benefits them and means nothing. But this can not be said of God. He is Faithful to His Nature—Love, Goodness, Righteousness and Justice.

1 John 1:9 says, *If we claim to be without sin, we deceive ourselves and the truth is not in us. If we confess our sins, he is faithful and just and will forgive us our sins and purify us from all unrighteousness.* We are promised that if we confess our sins, He is faithful and just to forgive and forget them. God knows we are not perfect, so His Mercy is new with every day. In His Faithfulness, He desires to forgive our sins and purify us from all unrighteousness. To purify means to wash clean, restore and make new again. Isaiah 1:18 says, *"Come now, let us reason together," says the LORD. "Though your sins are like scarlet, they shall be as white as snow; though they are red as crimson, they shall be like wool."* No matter what your mistakes or how often, they are never bigger than God's ability to forgive and purify us of our greatest sins. He is bigger than your sins and flaws. However, He desires that we

see them as they really are, confess them to Him and be made as white as snow. This is the Faithfulness of our God! Let us meditate on Psalm 136, the chapter dedicated to the Faithfulness of God:

> *Give thanks to the Lord, for he is good! His faithful love endures forever. Give thanks to the God of gods. His faithful love endures forever. Give thanks to the Lord of lords. His faithful love endures forever. Give thanks to him who alone does mighty miracles. His faithful love endures forever. Give thanks to him who made the heavens so skillfully. His faithful love endures forever. Give thanks to him who placed the earth among the waters. His faithful love endures forever. Give thanks to him who made the heavenly lights—His faithful love endures forever. The sun to rule the day, His faithful love endures forever and the moon and stars to rule the night. His faithful love endures forever . . . He remembered us in our weakness. His faithful love endures forever. He saved us from our enemies. His faithful love endures forever. He gives food to every living thing. His faithful love endures forever. Give thanks to the God of heaven. His faithful love endures forever.*
> —Psalm 136:1-9; 23-26 NIV, author's emphasis

Faithful is He who is Calling You

> *And may the God of peace Himself sanctify you through and through [separate you from profane things, make you pure and wholly consecrated to God]; and may your spirit and soul and body be preserved sound and complete [and found] blameless at the coming of our Lord Jesus Christ. Faithful is He who is calling you [to Himself] and utterly trustworthy, and He will also do it [fulfill His call by hallowing and keeping you].*
> —1 Thessalonians 5:23-24 NKJV, author's emphasis

The full meaning of this verse is that God is true and constant and will adhere to all of His promises. He will not promise and then fail to perform His words. He will not commence anything which He will not perfect and finish. And in this He is Faithful in calling you to Himself. And for us to come to Him we are to be holy and blameless in His presence. This He does with our participation through sanctifying and making holy. Though at times painful, challenging, unbearable and impossible, the end state is our glorification.

Now glorification describes our ultimate and complete conformity to the character and likeness of Jesus Christ. It is the final link in the great golden chain of our salvation. Paul speaks of this in his letter to the Romans:

> *For those whom He foreknew [of whom He was aware and loved beforehand], He also destined from the beginning [foreordaining them] to be molded into the image of His Son [and share inwardly His likeness], that He might become the firstborn among many brethren. And those whom He thus foreordained, He also called; and those whom He called, He also justified (acquitted, made righteous, putting them into right standing with Himself). And those whom He justified, He also glorified [raising them to a heavenly dignity and condition or state of being].*
> —Romans 8:29-30 AMP, author's emphasis

In God's Faithfulness He promises to bring us to Himself. This is made possible by our glorification. Whom God calls He justifies and glorifies. As sure as He gives grace, He will give glory. Whom He calls to His eternal glory He will make perfect. God, the caller of His people, will cause His calling not to fall short of its designed end. To preserve and present you blameless at the coming of Christ (Colossians 1:22).

Since we have been called by God into the fellowship of His Son, His Faithfulness of character would render it certain that we would be kept to eternal life. By His Faithfulness, we are confident that He who began the good work within us, will accomplish it, on that great day when Jesus Christ returns (Philippians 1:6). The Holy Spirit is the great change agent. He cleanses, washes, renews and restores—spirit, soul and body—to present you holy and blameless above reproach in His presence.

Faithful is He that called you into your sanctification, who has begun a good work of grace in your hearts, you may depend on His Faithfulness to complete it. God promises to sanctify His people because His faithfulness binds Him to fulfill His promises. God is Faithful to His word, His covenant and His promises. He is also Faithful to sanctify and cleanse His people from all their sins and to preserve them safe for entrance to His Eternal Kingdom and Glory.[3]

Paul's prayer to the Thessalonians was that they might be sanctified more perfectly, for the best are sanctified. His prayer is for you and me too. Therefore we should pray for and press toward complete Holiness. We should pray to God to perfect His work in us, till we are presented faultless before the throne of His glory. Anything less is not His best.

Nothing has burdened my heart more than the days I have felt unspeakable shame and guilt of being unfaithful to God. Days and weeks would go by and I would feel no different. Great shame and sadness would flood my heart. Only genuine confession and repentance would remove it in its entirety. This is to be alone behind closed doors, get down on your hands and knees and put your face to the ground, understanding the gravity of your transgressions towards God and their impact on others. This is why continual repentance before God and others is so essential. We confess our sins to God and our faults to man to keep ourselves accountable.

James 5:16 says, *Confess to one another therefore your faults (your slips, your false steps, your offenses, your sins) and pray [also] for one another, that you may be healed and restored [to a spiritual tone of mind and heart].* Disease is often greatly aggravated by the trouble of mind which arises from conscious guilt; and, in such a case, nothing will contribute more directly to recovery than the restoration of peace to the soul agitated by guilt and by the dread of a judgement to come. This may be secured by confession—confession made first to God, and then to those who are wronged. [4]

This is to stop us from becoming self-destructive, when we believe everyone is wrong and we are right. The hardest but safest place you can ever be is to be humble. This is to be the furthest place from pride, bitterness, unforgiveness and the enemy.

Our Response to God Faithfulness

You then, my son, be strong in the grace that is in Christ Jesus. And the things you have heard me say in the presence of many witnesses entrust to reliable men who will also be qualified to teach others. <u>Endure hardship with us like a good soldier of Christ Jesus</u>. No one serving as a soldier gets involved in civilian affairs—he wants to please his commanding officer. Similarly, if anyone competes as an athlete, he does not receive the victor's crown unless he competes according to the rules. The hardworking farmer should be the first to receive a share of the crops. Reflect on what I am saying, for the Lord will give you insight into all this.
—2 Timothy 2:1-7 NIV, author's emphasis

Today in the church, our homes, and at work, we are called to be faithful in all that we do. To be faithful in marriage, to be faithful in serving, to be faithful with our finances, to be faithful in our workplaces. To honour and obey those in authority above us. To love our parents who gave us life. *For whoever is faithful in the least will be faithful with much; but whoever is unfaithful in even the little, will be unfaithful with much* (Luke 16:10). Faithfulness is essentially all about character; who you really are when no one is watching. The conduct of a man will never outperform his character. A true Christian is not necessarily a great servant, a prayer warrior, disciple or healing evangelist. The greatest test is if they are faithful. If they are faithful in the little they will be faithful with much. And the opposite is always true.

In a world of unfaithfulness in marriage, business, entertainment and politics, we must stand strong and be faithful with what is in our hands. For we are like soldiers in a battlefield, responding to orders from our Commander and Chief. We are athletes in training, running the race of our life. And we are farmers sowing seeds, reaping harvests of salvations and disciples.

We do not care about the things of this world which are soon perishing and will fade away. 1 John 2:17 says, *This world is fading away, along with everything it craves. But if you do the will of God you will live forever.*

God spoke to me several years ago, telling me of what His end times army will look like: "*I have called you to bring home the lost, the broken, the wounded, the hurting, the lame, the sick, the rejects of the world, the outcasts of society . . . bring them to My House where they will become My disciples.*" It is God's Faithfulness that reaches out when the world pushes away. Many are called and few are chosen because God chooses the foolish things of this world to shame the wise.

> *So, dear brothers and sisters, work hard to <u>prove</u> that you really are among those God has <u>called</u> and <u>chosen</u>. Do these things [moral excellence, knowledge, self-control, patient endurance, godliness, brotherly affection, love for everyone], and you will <u>never fall away</u>. Then God will give you a grand entrance into the eternal Kingdom of our Lord and Saviour Jesus Christ.*
> —2 Peter 1:10-11 NLT, author's emphasis and notes

Peter was writing to Christians who had believed in false teaching that taught salvation is not dependant on good works, so they could live in any way they wanted. He corrected them saying if they truly belonged to Christ, to work hard to prove that they really were among those God had called and chosen. In other words, show me evidence of a changed and transformed life. Show me evidence of your faithfulness and obedience. Show me evidence of how you have multiplied your talents that God has given you. Prove it! His words are no less applicable to us today.

James echoes these sentiments by saying, *What good is it, dear brothers and sisters, if you say you have faith but don't show it by your actions? Can that kind of faith save anyone? . . . Now someone may argue, "Some people have faith; others have good deeds." But I say, "How can you show me your faith if you don't have good deeds? I will show you my faith by my good deeds" . . . Just as the body is dead without breath, so also faith is dead without good works* (James 2:14; 18; 26). Good works do not earn automatic salvation, but when done with the right heart, they are evidence of faithfulness that *brings* salvation.

God can not deny Himself, for that would be a denial of His very nature to save those who are unfaithful. He is Holy, so how can he save one who is unholy?

His very nature is Purity, so how can he save one who has no purity? Let no one, then, suppose that, because he is elected, he is safe if he lives in deliberate sin. The electing purpose of God, indeed, makes salvation sure but it is only for those who lead righteous lives. Nothing would be more dishonorable for God than to resolve to save a man that lived happily and unconcerned in his sin.[5]

1 Corinthians 1:20-21 says, *Where is the wise person? Where is the teacher of the law? Where is the philosopher of this age? Has not God made foolish the wisdom of the world? For since in the wisdom of God the world through its wisdom did not know him, God was pleased through the foolishness of what was preached to save those who believe.* A call to Faithfulness is shouting in the distance. God's army will be individuals of men and women of proven faithfulness to the end, tried and tested. Proven genuine in the fires of life. How about you, are you in?

> *If the Lord should bring a wicked man to heaven, heaven would be hell to him; for he who loves not grace upon earth will never love it in heaven.*
> Christopher Love, Welsh Protestant (1618-1651)

Faithfulness's Contemporary: God's Rejection

> *But I assure you of this: If you ever forget the Lord your God and follow other gods, worshiping and bowing down to them, you will certainly be destroyed. Just as the Lord has destroyed other nations in your path, <u>you also will be destroyed if you refuse to obey the Lord your God.</u>*
> —Deuteronomy 8:19-20 NIV, author's emphasis

This is a sobering and uncomfortable truth, but a necessary one. It is the highest treason to treat God's Faithfulness with disregard or contempt. To forget His Goodness, Mercy and past blessings towards us and to pursue something else over Him will not go unpunished. He tolerates no rivals, He is to be our only desire. God proves His Love by showing Mercy towards sinners, just as He demonstrates His Righteousness by His Judgement towards evil. Justice must be present in Judgement, just as Love must be present in Mercy. One attribute does not cancel out another of His divine characteristics. Likewise God's Faithfulness towards His true children is shown by His rejection of those who deny Him and the unfaithful. The responsibility to be faithful is always on us, never God.

For if we go on sinning deliberately after receiving the knowledge of the truth, there no longer remains a sacrifice for sins, but a fearful expectation of judgement, and a fury of fire that will consume the adversaries. Anyone who has set aside the law of Moses dies without mercy on the evidence of two or three witnesses. How much worse punishment, do you think, will be deserved by the one who has spurned the Son of God, and has profaned the blood of the covenant by which he was sanctified, and has outraged the Spirit of grace?
—Hebrews 10:26-29 NIV

The bible is full of warning signs against walking away from the faith. Sadly I can count more than a dozen people who I know personally who have chosen to walk away from God in the last several years. Whether they return I do not know, but great sadness and sorrow fills my heart. I know some who still attend church but are far from all they could be. They still live defeated lives, complaining and struggling every week, never changing or learning from their mistakes.

Some live in darkness and have seared their conscience, not knowing good from evil anymore (1 Timothy 4:2). Still others, who were the loudest and most noticeable in church when they started, soon left over a simple offence. They put their trust in man and looked to leaders instead of God for acceptance, appreciation and praise. A study in America found a number of startling statistics amongst church members that shows this is unfortunately all too common:

- 10% can not be found
- 20% never attend
- 25% never pray
- 30% never read the Bible
- 40% never give to church
- 60% never give to world missions

- 75% never assume a ministry service in the church
- 95% have never won one person to Christ, though
- 100% expect to go to Heaven.[6]

Many enjoy hearing about God's Faithfulness and promises of blessings and favour. But how many would respond by being faithful themselves? To sacrifice their time to be faithful in attending church, to faithfully pray for the needs of others, and to faithfully give sacrificially to worthy charities and building God's Kingdom on earth?

Many today are unfaithful in relationships, giving, and integrity at work. Many are unfaithful in honouring those in leadership, parents and their neighbour. Those who treat God's Faithfulness casually will by no means experience His blessings, but His rejection. It is clear that to forsake God and live in rebellion, disobedience and deliberate sin is high treason. Scriptures provides many examples of God's rejection towards His people who did evil and were unfaithful. In the Old Testament, God rejected:

- Cain's offering (Genesis 4:5);
- Judah's evil offerings (Malachi 1:6-14);
- Allowed Israel's enemies to conquer them when they turned away (Judges 2:10-19) and finally exiled from the Promised Land (2 Kings 25).

In the New Testament, Jesus spoke loud and clearly about the rejection of:

- The unfaithful servant (Luke 12:45-47);
- The five foolish virgins (Matthew 25:10-13);
- The unprofitable servant (Matthew 25:24-30);
- The unforgiving debtor (Matthew 18:28-35);
- On Judgement Day, He will separate the sheep, true believers, from the goats, false believers, (Matthew 25:41-46).

Psalm 50:16-22 says some powerful words at what God will say to those who should have known better: *But God says to the wicked: "Why bother reciting my decrees and pretending to obey my covenant? For you refuse my discipline and treat my words like trash. When you see thieves, you approve of them, and you spend your time with adulterers. Your mouth is filled with wickedness, and your tongue is full of lies. You sit around and slander your brother— your own mother's son. While you did all this, I remained silent, and you thought I didn't care. But now I will rebuke you, listing all my charges against you. Repent, all of you who forget me, or I will tear you apart, and no one will help you.*

It is clear that God has high standards for His people to be faithful. In Revelations Jesus rebukes five of the seven churches for compromise, sexual immorality and lukewarmness. There is much Grace given to us but with this Grace comes much expectation for faithfulness and fruitfulness. Jesus is coming back for a church without stain, wrinkle or any blemish, but holy and blameless (see Ephesians 5:25-27). He is coming back expecting us to be *faithful* in our talents, *faithful* in our marriages, *faithful* in serving where God has placed us and *faithful* in life.

If we are dead to this world, its pleasures, profits, and honours, we shall be forever with Christ in a better world. He is *faithful* to His warnings and *faithful* to His promises. This truth makes sure the unbeliever's condemnation and the believer's salvation.[7] God's Faithfulness in the midst of our continual unfaithfulness will not be tolerated forever. His judgement is always delayed but always certain. To those who are Faithful, they will see and touch His Faithfulness. But to those who are unfaithful, they will experience His terrifying rejection and wrath.

Example—Korah's Rebellion Against Moses

> *One day Korah son of Izhar, a descendant of Kohath son of Levi, conspired with Dathan and Abiram, the sons of Eliab, and On son of Peleth, from the tribe of Reuben. They incited a rebellion against Moses, along with 250 other leaders of the community, all prominent members of the assembly. They united against Moses and Aaron and said, "You have gone too far! The whole community of Israel has been set apart by the LORD, and he is with all of us. What right do you have to act as though you are greater than the rest of the LORD's people?"*
> —Numbers 16:1-3 NLT, author's emphasis

Moses was divinely chosen and prepared by God to lead His people out of Egypt into the Promised Land. Moses brother Aaron was also chosen to be the spiritual leader over all the people. The tribe of Levi was chosen to assist in temple duties and minister in the sanctuary. However, it wasn't long until a great complaint rose up within the ranks.

A Levite named Korah and his associates had seen the advantages of the priesthood in Egypt. Egyptian priests had great wealth and political influence, something greatly prized. Korah may have assumed that Moses and Aaron were trying to make the Israelite priesthood the same kind of political system, and he wanted in on the benefits. Korah already had significant abilities and responsibilities, but he wanted more. What's more he had much influence among the people and brought prominent leaders within the community against Moses and Aaron.

A twofold rebellion against Moses and Aaron erupts. Korah and his rebels wanted more power and Moses leadership. Their objection to Moses' authority was that he backed away from the Promised Land and returned to the wilderness and had not been successful in entering since. Korah charges Moses and Aaron with taking power and wealth for their own selfish purposes, despite miraculous signs that they were called by God to it. Moses sought instruction from God. They were now under the judgement of God who would defend Moses Himself.

And the LORD said to Moses, "Then tell all the people to get away from the tents of Korah, Dathan, and Abiram." So Moses got up and rushed over to the tents of Dathan and Abiram, followed by the elders of Israel. "Quick!" he told the people. "Get away from the tents of these wicked men, and don't touch anything that belongs to them. If you do, you will be destroyed for their sins." So all the people stood back from the tents of Korah, Dathan, and Abiram. Then Dathan and Abiram came out and stood at the entrances of their tents, together with their wives and children and little ones. And Moses said, "This is how you will know that the LORD has sent me to do all these things that I have done—for I have not done them on my own. If these men die a natural death, or if nothing unusual happens, then the LORD has not sent me. But if the LORD does something entirely new and the ground opens its mouth and swallows them and all their belongings, and they go down alive into the grave, then you will

*know that these men have shown contempt for the LORD." <u>He had hardly finished</u>
<u>speaking the words when the ground suddenly split open beneath them. The earth</u>
<u>opened its mouth and swallowed the men, along with their households and all their</u>
<u>followers who were standing with them, and everything they owned.</u> So they went down
alive into the grave, along with all their belongings. The earth closed over them, and
they all vanished from among the people of Israel.*
—Numbers 16:23-33 NLT, author's emphasis

Moses shows their privileges as Levites, and convicts them of the sin of
undervaluing these privileges. Moses saw through their accusations to their true
motives and pronounced judgement which God delivered—immediately. He
did not understand that Moses' main ambition was to serve God rather than
control others and acquire great power and wealth. Korah's pride and greed caused
him to lose everything. His influence was powerful and caused many lives to be
lost, including his family. He forgot everything God had given him and failed
to recognise the importance of the position God had placed him in. Korah was
blinded by a lust for power and accused Moses of the same. His deception cost
him dearly.

People want change but in reality they want *power*. Power hungry people who can't
wait for God's timing take matters into their own hands at their own peril. One
of the great temptations is to speak down on God's anointed leader, even if we are
right and somehow think they deserve it. But think again when you believe God
will honour your rebellion! God has the last say at the end of the day. He sees into
the hearts and motives of everyone. Nothing is hidden from His knowledge.

Pride and ambition cause a great deal of trouble in both church life and in general.
May we too be warned to keep us from envying those above us, and to honour
those greatly above us who God has charged to lead us faithfully. God has reserved
severe punishments for those who bring rebellion and disunity among His chosen
servants. The ruin of others should be a stern warning to us. Could we, by faith,
hear the cries of those that have gone down to the bottomless pit, we should give
more diligence than we do to escape for our lives, lest we also come into their
condemnation.[8]

Final Thoughts

To those who live for God, He won't abandon you. You are a child of God, created by Him. You are accepted and valued by Him. He is Faithful to sanctify you and turn you into Christ. Because God is Faithful, everything He does is good, perfect and divine.

Does it mean He no longer loves us if we have trouble or calamity, or are persecuted, or hungry, or destitute, or in danger, or threatened with death? . . . No, despite all these things, overwhelming victory is ours through Christ, who loved us
—Romans 8:35-37 NLT

God has not abandoned you, even in times of trouble, distress or persecution. Don't abandon your work, your dreams and God when things get tough. God is Faithful to those who are faithful, not necessarily the unfaithful and unbelieving. The fact that He is Faithful should be of greatest reassurance in itself.

CHAPTER 9

The Abundance of God

It would shock you if you knew how much God wants to bless you,
so you can be a carrier of blessings to others.

Now to Him who, by (in consequence of) the [action of His] power that is at work within us, is able to [carry out His purpose and] do <u>superabundantly, far over and above all that we [dare] ask or think</u> [infinitely beyond our highest prayers, desires, thoughts, hopes, or dreams].

—Ephesians 3:20 AMP, author's emphasis

I was speaking in Kansas City to a well-known large church. I shared a testimony about how I was in a desperate situation financially. I had heard about the $58 seed teaching only weeks earlier; $1 representing the 58 specific blessings on prosperity in the Bible. At the time it was a huge stretch but I did it. Very soon, my circumstances began to change and finances miraculously came my way.

After the service a little boy walked up to me. I had no idea what his name was or anything about his background. But the Holy Spirit spoke to my heart, 'Give him a $100 bill'. I was shocked! 'He's too little', I reasoned. I could give him $10 and he would be just as excited. The Holy Spirit insisted. So I reached inside my pocket, rather reluctantly and discretely handed him a $100 bill. A few minutes later a little girl walked up to me. It was his sister. I did not know her name and still do not know to this day. The Holy Spirit said again 'Give her a $100 bill also'. If I was shocked before I was green now! What's going on? I'm not going to have anything left in the next five minutes! The Holy Spirit nudged me again. But I knew that this was the voice of the Holy Spirit. I obeyed and handed her a $100 bill from my wallet.

Suddenly a woman walked up to us. It turned out that she was their mother and a believer. She was stunned when she saw her two children waving $100 bills at her with huge smiles on their faces. She blurted out, 'What is this for?' A little hesitantly I said, 'The Holy Spirit told me to give it to them'. She struggled to contain herself and then began to cry.

After composing herself she said, 'Tonight you told every one of us to plant a seed of $58 to represent the 58 blessings in the Bible. When I went through my purse with tears in my eyes, I was so disheartened. You see, my husband left me three weeks ago. He has refused to help us financially at all. When the children and I came to church tonight, we did not have a can of food in our pantry. No milk in the refrigerator. No food at all. We are broke! When I emptied my purse during the offering, I looked for every penny I could find, every nickel, to find the $58 dollars. I did not have it. But, the total amount of money that I found in my purse was 58 cents. So, I prayed 'Lord, I am planting this 58 cents as a memorial that I want you to remember me. I have confidence you're going to bless me will all 58 blessings'. She kept crying. She said, 'Now my children and I can go to an all-night grocery store and buy $200 worth of groceries for our family'.

I can't tell you how much that blessed and lifted my heart. You see, my $200 was my harvest God had provided for me recently. I had no idea that I could create a forever memory in a small family who lacked food and desperately needed a demonstration of God's goodness in their life. That I was the answer to her prayer and that God remembered her. You can not believe how powerful your harvest can be until you concentrate on the good it can do for others . . . [1]

We serve a God of Abundance on every level. The world we live in is a paradise of colour, detail, beauty and power. Even if we only lived in black and white, life would still be amazing. When you see the creation, you catch a glimpse of the heart and mind of the Creator. Ephesians 3:20 says God is able to do *superabundantly, far over and above all that we [dare] ask or think*. Simply nothing is impossible with God. He can do anything, anywhere, anytime. He speaks the universe into being, parts oceans, brings down fortified walls and raises the dead. Doing the impossible is what God does best. All we have to do is simply believe He can do it.

Additionally, Strong defines abundance in the Greek as *perissos*, meaning *overflowing, surplus, over and above, more than enough, above the ordinary, more than sufficient.*[2] When Jesus said He came to give us life and life more abundantly, He fully meant that we would have overflowing and more than enough in every area of our lives! This was achieved by His work on the Cross. Our sins were forgiven, relationship with God restored and the gift of the Holy Spirit was sent to us to rule in our hearts and reign in our life. The curse of sin, the law and especially poverty was broken off us. We now have unrestricted access to heaven's treasures, including all spiritual and physical resources.

Salvation is the Greek word for *sozo* which means 'save'. It occurs over 100 times in the New Testament. Interestingly, most of the references refer to our present physical condition rather than our spiritual salvation. It is a total package—victory in life, peace in our mind, joy in our heart, healing for our body, forgiveness for our soul and prosperity in material possessions. Now that's good news!

And God shall supply all of my needs, according to His riches and glory in Christ
—Philippians 4:19 NIV

A common misperception is that abundance is limited to finances only. But if that was the case then that would be a raw deal! Abundance is not at all limited to finances but to *every* area of our lives; emotionally, spiritually, relationally, in work, hobbies, hopes, dreams and desires. God doesn't want you to be satisfied with burnt toast and soggy Weetbix. He wants you to be satisfied with the finest crab and French champagne! Not so you can just keep it all to yourself, but so that you would have enough for all those around you in need. Believe for yourself today that it is God's will to bless you, not just financially but in all areas for your life. It would shock you if you knew how much God wants to bless you, so you can be a carrier of blessings to others. For God will supply all of our needs with plenty left over to bless others.

The Nature of God is to Show Abundance

For you know the grace of our Lord Jesus Christ, that though he was rich, yet for your sake he became poor, so that you through his poverty might become rich.
—2 Corinthians 8:9 NIV

The full meaning of this verse is Jesus was willing to step down from His exalted position in heaven and receive the curse of poverty at the Cross so that we could become rich. Though He was rich, yet for our sakes He became poor. Christ parted with riches and took poverty; with glory and took humiliation; with bliss and took suffering. If He gave Himself for us, what shall we give for Him? Nothing less than what He gave to us.[3]

God's covenant is a covenant of Abundance. He wanted man to be prosperous from the very beginning. Never doubt or think otherwise—our God is a God of Abundance. It is to have all prosperity to the person in soul and body, to the family, wife, children, and there estate, cattle, farms, fields, vineyards, and all that belongs to them. To the degree that a more extensive blessing could simply not be made.[4]

The thief comes only in order to steal and kill and destroy. [But] I came that they may have and enjoy life, and have it in abundance (to the full, till it overflows).
—John 10:10 AMP, author's emphasis

Jesus mission statement was for us to have *life and life more abundantly!* This is God's desire for your life too—more than you can dare to imagine! Jesus told us in no uncertain terms that His purpose in coming to earth was so you and I could have a life in abundance. Not a life of lack, or just getting by, overflow and more than enough! It is the devil who wants every area of our life to be destroyed. He hates God and everything He represents. Because we are made in His image, every time he sees us he sees the image of God. His mission statement is to kill, steal and destroy everything you are and everything you have. He wants to steal your joy, peace, possessions and friends. Then he wants to kill your relationships, career, hopes and dreams. Finally, he desires to destroy your life and eternity without

God. But he is defeated and has no power when Christ lives and dwells in our hearts, who defeated him at the Cross.

God's Abundance to His people comes in many types and ways. It is not limited to only finances or material wealth as many falsely believe. If that is all we had abundance in, we would be greatly disappointed! Scripture shows us that God's Abundance is shown in His Grace being exceedingly abundant (1 Timothy 1:14), His forgiveness being abundant (Isaiah 55:7), and His mercy being abundant every day (Nehemiah 9:27). For a father to have poor, sick and dirty children is a sign of a bad father which reflects his values and character. But a father who has privileged, healthy and clean children is a father of great love and compassion. This is *exactly* the heart of God—that you would live well have everything you need and extra to share around. For every good and perfect gift comes from the Father above who is in Heaven (James 1:17).

According to God's word your future is getting brighter and you are on your way to a new level of glory! Romans 8:30 says, *And those he predestined, he also called; those he called, he also justified; those he justified, he also glorified.* Your value to God has already been determined. You were bought back with Jesus' blood, the highest price in the universe! God wants you to increase, to prosper, and to be blessed in every way. Not always in our timing and methods but in His perfect timing and ways.

Our responsibility is to simply believe in our heart and speak it out in faith. Wrong thinking can keep us from God's best. You can't afford the power of a negative, self-critical thought life. Your life will never change until you change your thinking. Start with believing God wants you to live a life of abundance. Nothing is impossible with God, but He is limited by our lack of faith and unbelief. God always meets us at our level of faith and thinking. Jesus said over and over again to the people, *According to your faith, let it be done for you.* According to the expectation and belief that you think God can do whatever the impossible you ask for, you can have. I encourage you if you haven't already, start believing and speaking for God's Abundance for your life today. You will be amazed at what He has in store for you.

'I wish above all things . . .'

I wish above all things that you may prosper and be in health, even as your soul prospers.

—3 John 2 NKJV

The apostle John wished earnestly *above all things* that you would prosper just as your soul prospers. His love and concern for his family in Christ was so that they would have everything they needed in life. When your soul prospers, every area of our life prospers—finances, emotions, health and relationships. This includes success in business, happiness in relationships, or profit in any transactions you might lawfully engage. Soul prosperity is the greatest blessing on this side of heaven. Grace and health are good friends and rich companions.

Anyone who criticises prosperity must therefore disagree with the Word of God which is to say God is wrong. Anyone who rejects God's Word rejects Him and Jesus because His Word is His bond, and Jesus is the Word made flesh (John 1:14). They must also believe somehow Jesus got it wrong too, because Jesus said He came to give us *life* and *life more abundantly*. Those who disagree with God's Word must therefore believe that it is not right that we can be saved. This is outrageous! Prospering in life has been God's intent since the very beginning, and is still applicable to us today. To think otherwise is to be greatly deceived. Consider the following for people not to believe in prosperity but still believe in the Bible:

1) **They must agree that it was wrong that Joseph prospered:**
   Genesis 39:2—*The LORD was with Joseph and he prospered, and he lived in the house of his Egyptian master* (NIV).

2) **They must agree that it was wrong that David prospered:**
   1 Samuel 18:14—*David was prospering in all his ways for the LORD was with him* (NASB).

3) **They must agree that it was wrong that Daniel prospered:**
Daniel 6:28—*So Daniel prospered during the reign of Darius and the reign of Cyrus the Persian* (NIV).

4) **They must agree that it is wrong that we should prosper when we are planted in the House of God:**
Psalms 1:3—*They are like trees planted along the riverbank, bearing fruit each season. Their leaves never wither, and they prosper in all they do* (NLT).

5) **They must agree that it is wrong that when we trust God, we shouldn't prosper:**
Proverbs 28:25—*A greedy man stirs up dissension, but he who trusts in the LORD will prosper* (NIV).

6) **They must agree that it is wrong that we should prosper when we are strong and courageous, doing everything necessary to obey God's Word:**
Joshua 1:7—*Only be strong and very courageous, that you may observe to do according to all the law which Moses My servant commanded you; do not turn from it to the right hand or to the left, that you may prosper wherever you go* (NKJV).

7) **And they must agree that it is wrong that God said He had good plans for us to prosper:**
Jeremiah 29:11—*For I know the plans I have for you," declares the LORD, "plans to prosper you and not to harm you, plans to give you hope and a future"* (NIV).

And we could go on and on. It is simply absurd to believe that God does not desire for us to prosper in life. To believe that lie is to believe God in His perfection and glory is wrong! Friend, it is the lie of the enemy that we should not prosper. He does not want us to have more than enough to help other people in need. He does not want us to give to charities and those in need. And he definitely does not want us to give to the Kingdom of God, giving finances to spread the gospel and see the lost come to Christ. Money is a weapon against the kingdom of darkness. He knows just how powerful finances are to the local church.

Abundance and Blessings Follow Obedience

*For the LORD God is a sun and shield; the LORD bestows favour and honor;
no good thing does he withhold from those whose walk is blameless.*
—Psalms 84:11 NIV

It is clear blessings follow closely behind obedience to God's ways. When our life is honouring Him and you are obeying all of His instructions, it is guaranteed that favour and honour will soon follow. God is the rewarder of our faith. He desires to reward our efforts and encourage us in our faith. It is the Greatness of God that brings blessings, not our personal greatness.

Abundance comes through our channel of living a life in Christ. All the favours that Paul expected for himself and his fellow man, he believed would be given to us through our Redeemer. In Genesis 1, God gave us the world to have a life of all things to enjoy, bountifully and abundantly. Furthermore, God gave His Son so we could have joy in all things freely, in whom we are redeemed, accepted and saved. Nothing less than *exceedingly abundantly above all you could ever possibly ask or think!*

Biblical prosperity verses simply abound throughout scripture when a life of obedience follows. To prosper and live a life of abundance is promised many times over. It is no accident that many of the famous men of faith who achieved extraordinary things were very rich and prosperous. They were all known to obey God's ways carefully. Job, Abraham, Moses, David and Solomon God prospered them greatly:

1) **Job**—Job was very wealthy and owned many cattle and servants. *The LORD blessed the latter part of Job's life more than the first. He had fourteen thousand sheep, six thousand camels, a thousand yoke of oxen and a thousand donkeys* (Job 42:12).

2) **Abraham**—Abraham was also very wealthy with much livestock, riches and servants. *Abram was very rich in livestock, in silver and gold* (Genesis 13:2).

3) **Moses**—Moses and Aaron received the tithes of all the priests who had received the tithes of all the people (Numbers 18:28). There were 600,000 men at that time. If say two thirds of them were employed at $250 weekly, that's a $25 tithe multiplied by 400,000, which equals $10 million. The tithe of this would be $1 million which adds up to $52 million a year! This is very possible because they plundered Egypt before they left for the wilderness.[5]

4) **King David**—David was extraordinarily wealthy, so much that he was able to give all of his resources to build the temple. *I now give my personal treasures of gold and silver for the temple of my God, over and above everything I have provided for this holy temple: three thousand talents of gold (gold of Ophir) and seven thousand talents of refined silver, for the overlaying of the walls of the buildings* (1 Chronicles 29:3-4). This was 110 tonnes of gold and 220 tonnes of silver, totalling today's standards approximately $2.8 billion.

5) **King Solomon**—Solomon invited the Queen of Sheba to his palace who was breathtaken at the expansive wealth he had accumulated. *When the queen of Sheba saw all the wisdom of Solomon and the palace he had built, the food on his table, the seating of his officials, the attending servants in their robes, his cupbearers, and the burnt offerings he made at the temple of the LORD, she was overwhelmed. . . . The weight of the gold that Solomon received yearly was 666 talents, [25 tonnes] not including the revenues from merchants and traders and from all the Arabian kings and the governors of*

the land . . . King Solomon was greater in riches and wisdom than all the other kings of the earth. The whole world sought audience with Solomon to hear the wisdom God had put in his heart. Year after year, everyone who came brought a gift—articles of silver and gold, robes, weapons and spices, and horses and mules (1 Kings 10:4-5; 14-15; 23-25). Estimates of the total of all of Solomon's wealth have been roughly estimated by some at one trillion dollars.

6) **Paul**—being a former Pharisee Paul would have been very wealthy. He travelled Asia Minor three times with a companion and could afford a Roman trial. When Paul was kept in prison for two years by the Roman procurator Felix, he hoped for a bribe from the apostle and would not have waited so long for a small amount (Acts 24:26). He knew Paul could deliver. Additionally, Paul tells Philemon to put on his account anything the runaway slave Onesimus owed him, confident he could pay any amount.

Prosperity is a way of living and thinking, and not just money or things. Likewise poverty is a way of living and thinking, and not just a lack of money or things.
—Eric Butterworth, minister and author (1917-2003)

Opening the Windows of Heaven over your Life

Bring the whole tithe into the storehouse, that there may be food in my house. Test me in this," says the LORD Almighty, "and <u>see if I will not throw open the floodgates of heaven and pour out so much blessing that you will not have room enough for it</u>. I will prevent pests from devouring your crops, and the vines in your fields will not cast their fruit," says the LORD Almighty. "Then all the nations will call you blessed, for yours will be a delightful land," says the LORD Almighty.
—Malachi 3:10-12 NIV, author's emphasis

Scripture is clear that God's Abundance and blessings come with an open heaven over our lives when we give our tithes and offerings. Malachi 3 is one of the greatest promises in scripture which speaks specifically of this. It does not hide the fact that finances are one of the major keys to unlocking the Abundance of God in our lives. Here we see three divine promises and blessings simply by obedience to tithing:

1) *'See if I will not throw open the floodgates of heaven . . .'* —favour, blessings, joy and good fortune will follow you. God's riches need to go to someone, why not you?

2) *'I will prevent pests from devouring your crops . . . '*—reproach the enemy off your life, financially, relationally, emotionally, spiritually. A hedge of protection will cover you wherever you go.

3) *'Yours will be a delightful land . . . '*—your place of residence will prosper and be blessed, you will enjoy the fruit of your labours, free from droughts and storms that might impede against producing income and profitability.

Giving is so important because it displays the character of God living in you. It honours Him and shows you place God as number one in your life. An honorarium is to present a gift worthy of the one who it is given to. How much more God, who is the King of Kings, Creator of heaven and earth! Not only does He promise His blessing on His people, He challenges us to prove Him and put Him to the test! Nowhere else are we permitted to test God in such a manner. As Christians we have the opportunity to use our finances to build God's Kingdom in two ways:

1) Tithes—giving to God what already belongs to Him, the first tenth of our income

2) Offerings—anything extra we give out of an overflow of our love for God

Now, tithing is not spare change when your conscience bothers you. It should be a regular discipline and premeditated. It is a lifestyle, a passion and a *conviction* inside of you that no one can shake you from. Arguments that say 'tithing was only required under the law' are hugely mistaken. The tithe was established hundreds of years well before the law by Abraham.

After Abram returned from defeating Kedorlaomer and the kings allied with him, the king of Sodom came out to meet him in the Valley of Shaveh (that is, the King's Valley). Then Melchizedek king of Salem brought out bread and wine. He was priest of God Most High, and he blessed Abram, saying, "Blessed be Abram by God Most High, Creator of heaven and earth. And blessed be God Most High, who delivered your enemies into your hand." Then Abram gave him a tenth of everything.
—Genesis 14:17-20 NIV

Additionally, many places in the New Testament refer to tithing and giving generously on all occasions. Let us not forget that life is short and money is just a test of true riches in heaven. Jesus said, *Do not store up for yourselves treasures on earth, where moth and rust destroy, and where thieves break in and steal. But store up for yourselves treasures in heaven, where neither moth nor rust destroys, and where thieves do not break in or steal. For where your treasure is, there your heart will be also* (Matthew 6:19-21).

Your treasure is what you value, spend time and honour which is the greatest sign of where your heart is. Money is a great testing ground for locating a person's priorities. Our hearts are always in either one of two places: on God or on ourselves. I encourage you, give cheerfully, willingly and obediently, and see the floodgates of heaven open on your life!

Our Response to God's Abundance

Every man shall give as he is able, according to the blessing of the LORD your God which He has given you.
—Deuteronomy 16:17 NIV

This abundance is not just for us so we can call ourselves blessed and become rich and fat. It is to give to others so we can abound in every good work. Money especially is at most times a great problem solver in helping struggling people in need. Even if prosperity is not a subject you enjoy listening to, what about all the family and friends struggling around you? What about the homeless who sleep on park benches in your city? And what about starving children overseas who have nothing because of famine and civil war? If you had more resources, wouldn't you really wish you could help them in a significant way? This is the other side of the coin of God's Abundance: not merely being blessed but becoming *an instrument of blessing* to others in great need. May we never become like the rich Pharisee who neglected the needs of Lazarus at his front gate daily and did nothing. Though he had the power and resources to take action he selfishly refused and held back from his abundance (see Luke 16:19-31). Excuses of ignorance, complacency or busyness will not stand before God.

Hoarding any type of excess blessings for yourself which should be given to those in need is a sin. It is a sin to have abundance and to withhold when we could meet the immediate needs of others. This is when James warns, *The very wealth you were counting on . . . will stand as evidence against you on the day of judgement* (5:3). Our response is to always give as you are able according to the blessings God has given you. This is especially the case when it is out of our overflow, which displays the nature of God within us. It always comes back to us in faith in ways we can never imagine.

Many times I have been stretched to give financially and seen incredible results. When I was twenty I had the dream of opening a stall at my local markets and being successful. After much research I decided that the best niche idea that was currently not being done was selling pancakes. So, full of enthusiasm and energy I launched myself into getting everything ready. I used up all of my savings and bought a flat top BBQ, eskis, drinks, pancake ingredients and a gazebo. I committed to one market day a month from the start of the year.

The first day arrived and it was a complete disaster! Being the month of January no one had money to spend after Christmas. Only three hours into the day the weather changed dramatically and a huge wind storm blew in knocking over my gazebo and all customers driving straight home. Furthermore, I had over stocked terribly and had tonnes of stock that would soon expire before the next market day!

The next month I changed locations and did better but didn't make as much money as I would have liked. The third market day was steaming hot and standing up all day without a break smelling like pancakes wasn't worth any money on my weekend off! Finally, I had had enough and decided to call it quits. I had spent $1,800 all up and was far from breaking even. I thought I had made the worst mistake of my life. I had been a Christian for a year at the time so I prayed, *Father, I will believe you can turn this situation around. Please guide me and give me wisdom so I can get back my savings.*

That Sunday at church was the weekend of my birthday. At the time I had been given some money and just happened to carry cash with me. I was very new at giving to church and didn't give all too much. When the offering time came I felt the Holy Spirit tell me to put in a $50 dollar note. I objected! *What for? That's ten times what I'm currently giving!* But after some thought I decided to give it a go and see if it would come back by faith. It was the best decision I ever made. The following weekend was market day. I had the idea that week to put up signs, '*Pancake Stall for Sale*'.

The place was packed, business was booming and the weather was perfect. Everyone was hungry that day for just one thing: pancakes! Word got out that I was selling cans of drink for half price, something unprecedented before and not recommended. But the best was yet to come. A man came up and enquired about the sale of the stall. We negotiated and I sold him everything that day! When adding up all the money I had broken even and got back exactly all of my savings, $1,800! Needless to say I was absolutely ecstatic and over the moon.

Another time I was travelling the United States for four months doing the Camp America program in Seattle, WA. Being established in tithing and earning some money as a camp counselor, I made a pre-determined decision to give my 10% and give a $20 offering every week I was away. Not the best decision while travelling overseas mind you when money is tight. But I believed God would provide for me if I was faithful in this one area. I had sold my car to pay for a two week tour and had some money saved away for when I got back to get a second hand one.

During the trip most weekends I was unable to make a church service, so I carefully put money aside and documented my giving. Some weeks I had second thoughts thinking, *this is crazy, what are you doing? That's a lot of money your giving right there. You might need it to pay for accommodation, food and travelling. You're not working for two-and-a-half months remember?* But God was Faithful. Everywhere I travelled I was either staying at camp, friends of camp, family or friends of family. I offered to pay for board everywhere I travelled but they all flatly refused.

Finally at the end of my trip I calculated that I only ever paid for two nights' accommodation over four months travelling. Amazing! But it doesn't end there. When I got home I needed a car. As it turned out the family business was upgrading their cars and were looking for worthy family members to give two or three away. And guess who received a $10,000 second hand 2000 Ford sedan for free? You guessed it. I will never forget it for as long as I live. I am convinced that it all came back to that one act of obedience, stretch of faith and sacrifice in my giving.

We are to give as we are able according to the blessings God has given us. And out of our abundance we can abound in every good work. If you want something you've never had, you've got to do something you've never done. Remember, God is the rewarder of our faith (Hebrews 11:6). He won't ask you of something you couldn't do. The windows of heaven open over your life when you believe nothing is impossible with God and you obey His Word. It's not complicated or rocket science. It's just faith in a Great God.

Abundance's Contemporary: Poverty

> *One man gives freely, yet gains even more;*
> *another withholds unduly, but comes to poverty.*
> —Proverbs 11:24 NIV

Poverty is a great evil in the world today. No one truly believes poverty in any context or environment is good or necessary. It is important to understand that poverty is a *spirit*. It happens inside of us before it materialises around us. Poverty will make you doubt every good thing about yourself. It will make you question God's Goodness and His ability to be our Provider. Jesus broke the curse of poverty at the Cross on your behalf. Never let poverty thinking ever become a lifestyle or something to accept. That you don't feel worthy enough or that lack is okay.

It must be noted that a sign of poverty is not always a sign of God's displeasure at us or sin. But it is definitely not a permanent life of living God wants us to accept. Likewise abundance and prosperity is not a sign of living pleasing to God. Often a person's wealth is what keeps them from the Kingdom of God. Revelation 3:17-18 says, *You say, 'I am rich; I have acquired wealth and do not need a thing.' But you do not realise that you are wretched, pitiful, poor, blind and naked. I counsel you to buy from me gold refined in the fire, so you can become rich; and white clothes to wear, so you can cover your shameful nakedness; and salve to put on your eyes, so you can see.*

Jesus warned that it is very hard for a rich man to enter heaven if his wealth is the focus and what he places his trust in (Matthew 19:24). Poverty is not limited to finances; it can come in many ways and forms. We can be poor in relationships, poor in success, poor in health and struggle through life and just getting by. Poverty generally comes when there is disobedience to God's Word. The curse for breaking God's commandments is threefold: poverty, sickness, and the death.

Some believers question if God wants us to live in prosperity and abundance. There is a lie that has been around for centuries that God wants us to be in lack with the approval from a religious spirit of poverty. But nothing could be further from the truth. This is to say that Jesus lied and really said '*The devils aim is to kill, steal and destroy and I have come that he may fulfill that purpose!*' Ridiculous! Feeling guilty about having prosperity and abundance is a mindset that needs to go!

Then there are some 'well-meaning Christians' who think God inflicts poverty upon His children so that they will live a life of humility. You don't have to be broke in order to be humble! Anyone can be rich and humble and poor but full of pride. God will never put you in the pit of poverty to make you humble. He doesn't work that way. God in His Greatness is a God of Abundance.

Example—The Curse of Poverty: Neglecting the Tithe

"I the LORD do not change. So you, O descendants of Jacob, are not destroyed. Ever since the time of your forefathers you have turned away from my decrees and have not kept them. Return to me, and I will return to you," says the LORD Almighty. "But you ask, 'How are we to return?' "Will a man rob God? Yet you rob me. "But you ask, 'How do we rob you?' "In tithes and offerings. You are under a curse—the whole nation of you—because you are robbing me.

—Malachi 3:7-9 NIV, author's emphasis

Is tithing outdated? What happens when people do tithe? Or more importantly, what happens when we don't tithe? Understanding tithes and offerings is essential to understanding the heart of God and the blessings that can come into our world. The word 'tithe' literally means *tenth*—a universal measurement for all people to give a portion of their income to build God's Kingdom through the local church. Scripture is clear that to hold back the tithe is to rob God what belongs to Him.

God calls man cursed for stealing what divinely belongs to Him. People's hands are tied many times by their own poverty. Those who withhold their tithes are ultimately robbing themselves of the blessings of God. Ultimately, everything you possess first came from God. You came into this world with nothing and you will leave with nothing. It is therefore expected to give back a portion of what first belongs to Him out of obedience and faith. We are privileged to have the opportunity to respond and take part in God's greater purposes. God gives all people the opportunity of a lifetime: to participate in building the Kingdom of God. A Kingdom that can not be shaken and will endure forever. We are called to simply be stewards of what has been given to us and administer it responsibly.

The tithe you give never really leaves your life. It simply leaves your hand and goes into your future where it multiplies. Some are thinking about the limitations of their salary instead of the potential of their faith.

—Mike Murdoch, evangelist, pastor, author [6]

What is startling is that the more money people have, the less they tend to give. The enemy can't stop the return of Christ who robbed him of his power. But he can limit the work of the spread of the gospel until He comes. Millions of souls are at stake and our faithfulness in our giving is *essential.* We can prevent the building of God's Kingdom by withholding what belongs to Him. I remember hearing a message by Bobbie Houston from Hillsong Church conference years ago that really stuck with me: '*The gospel is free, but it costs a lot of money.'* For the church to spread the gospel and reach communities and transform nations can not be done with black and white newsletters, second class technology and hired out rooms from the local surf club. It must be done with excellence, sacrifice and determination to honour God in everything we do. We are all in this together and must give an account of our stewardship to the greatest cause on planet earth—the building of the local church to see people come to Jesus Christ.

Where are your Priorities?

Jesus sat down opposite the treasury, and began observing how the people were putting money into the treasury . . .
—Luke 12:41NLT

Scripture records that Jesus took the time and watched the people putting money into the treasury. Heaven misses nothing. We are responsible to bring our tithes and offerings faithfully to the House of God. Everything you give is noticed and recorded in heaven. In the bible, time after time, God blessed and prospered his faithful servants who excelled in the discipline of giving. You can pick just about anyone from scripture and you will see examples of God's blessing in their lives. Alternatively, for every unfaithful or disobedient individual you will find some kind of lack or curse on those who kept it back.

Give, and it will be given to you. They will pour into your lap a good measure, pressed down, shaken together, and running over. For by your standard of measure it will be measured to you in return.
—Luke 6:38 NIV

Jesus knew that there is a close connection between people's money and their hearts. Each man is to give what he has. *Equal sacrifice* not equal giving. When you invest your money in something, your heart will follow. Where your treasure is there your hearts and thoughts are also (Luke 12:34).

> *Churches in the United States received $4 billion in 1964. A survey showed there were 112 million Americans who claimed religious affiliations in that year. If they had tithed their 10%, it would have reached an estimated $25 billion. That means at least $21 billion was missing from Jesus Christ—their Saviour, Lord and King, that year.* [7]

One of the main resources holding back the church is finances. Buildings need to be built, pastors need to be paid, bills are always expensive and conferences need money to be run. Without the faithful giving of church members the message of the gospel will never spread where it is needed most. Each man is to give what he has and be faithful in his little. To put our hand to the plow and not look back. Millions of people's salvations are at stake and we must give an account on how we handled what God has temporarily given to us. Much is at stake.

In 1964, how many more people would have been saved? How many more disciples would have been made? Or how much enemy ground would have been taken back if that $21 billion would have been invested in the church that year? God knows exactly and He will demand an account from every individual who withheld what belonged to Him.

> *Why are you living in luxurious houses while my house lies in ruins? This is what the Lord of Heaven's Armies says: Look at what's happening to you! You have planted much but harvest little. You eat but are not satisfied. You drink but are still thirsty. You put on clothes but can not keep warm. Your wages disappear as though you were putting them in pockets filled with holes! . . . Now go up into the hills, bring down timber, and rebuild my house. Then I will take pleasure in it and be honored . . .*
> —Haggai 1:4-8 NLT

When Israel returned from exile and started re-building the nation, at one point they neglected the house of God while beautifying their houses. The foundation of the temple had been laid fourteen years before and some progress had been made in the building. But it had been laying in an unfinished state and forgotten. The people could find time to build their own luxurious houses and no longer saw God's temple as something of importance. As a result they were planting seeds but not harvesting. Eating and drinking but not satisfied. Their clothes were not keeping them warm and their money was disappearing. God told them that there was a direct connection and were under a curse.

God can not overwrite His laws. Time has not changed and God can not tolerate His work being stopped for lack of funds when His people are working on their own selfish desires. He warns us to consider our ways and examine our faith. Many good works have been intended and started, but it is not good enough when they are incomplete. Whatever God will take pleasure in we also ought to take pleasure in doing.[8]

David said, "My son Solomon is young and inexperienced, and the house to be built for the LORD should be of great magnificence and fame and splendor in the sight of all the nations. Therefore I will make preparations for it." So David made extensive preparations before his death.
—1 Chronicles 22:5 NIV, author's emphasis

The House of God must be our highest priority. That it would be a place of beauty, magnificence, excellence and greatness. It would reflect God and Heaven. To David and Solomon the building of God's temple was their heart's desire. This is why the psalmist says, *They are abundantly satisfied with the fullness of Your house, and You give them drink from the river of Your pleasures* (36:8, author's emphasis). This must be our hearts desire too. Only then will we be abundantly satisfied and drink from God's eternal pleasures.

Final Thoughts

We should always be ready to give on every occasion because God has given so much to us. How we can be the answer to someone else's prayers. This is the greatest joy of receiving God's abundance. That we would know what it means to be blessed to give than to receive. Jesus said clearly, *Whoever can be trusted with very little can also be trusted with much . . . If you have not been trustworthy in handling worldly wealth, who will trust you with true riches?* (Luke 16:10-11).

In order for God to trust you with more riches, you need to be faithful in the little. It's not a greed principle but a Biblical universal principle. Money is just a test of true riches in heaven. Tithing is proof of our faith and that we have conquered the spirit of greed. Man hoards, the devil steals, but God gives. Most importantly, you are a channel of God's blessing to others. This is the greatest place we can truly be in life.

CONCLUSION

I trust this book has stirred you to the Greatness of our God. Whenever times get tough, I pray that the knowledge of God's true nature will anchor you to stay strong in the midst of the storm.

Trusting God's character is paramount for a lifelong relationship with Him. Life is challenging and at times impossible. Sometimes He is distant and quiet, watching to see how we respond. This is because *there is a time for everything, and a season for every activity under heaven* (Ecclesiastes 3:1). There is a purpose in every season. In times of adversity and trials, when your foundation in God is strong you understand its purpose. You never once think God is against me and doesn't love or has forgotten me. Focus on God and His Greatness, never your lack or what you don't yet have.

This book is just the beginning of knowing the Greatness of God. I highly recommend you do your own personal study for yourself on these and others. As your knowledge and understanding of God deepens, so will your love and relationship with Him will deepen. Among some of His other popular characteristics that deserve their own book include His:

- Holiness
- Wisdom
- Eternity
- Glory
- Justice
- Self-sufficiency
- And many more

You, therefore, must be perfect [<u>growing into complete maturity of godliness in mind</u>
<u>and character</u>, having reached the proper height of virtue and integrity], as your
heavenly Father is perfect.
—Matthew 5:45 AMP, authors emphasis

Before we finish I want to emphasise one final point. We are to grow into perfection, just as God is perfect. This is not to be flawless and without sin. It is to *complete maturity of godliness in mind and character*. God needs Christians who are strong, wise, and to be mature in faith and integrity. He needs men and women of God who are faithful and obedient to His leading, prepared to sacrifice and spread the gospel. He is looking for believers who will step into the ranks of God's army and ready to fight the devil and his angels for a lost humanity. God's Greatness is not so we can live comfy, convenient, pain free lives. Lukewarmness, disobedience and a lifestyle of excuses are unacceptable. We are called to live in victory and freedom!

One of my favourite worship songs of all time is Hillsong's *The Greatness of Our God* (2010) by Darlene Zschech. This song has spoken into the depths of my soul and spirit countless times when going through extreme troubles and adversity. It speaks so clearly and beautifully of everything God is and everything we are. I hope it blesses you and speaks to you just the same.

(Chorus)
And no words can say, or song convey,
All You are, the Greatness of our God.
I spend my life to know, and I'm far from close
To all You are, the Greatness of our God.

REFERENCES

Chapter 1—The Greatness of our God

1. Webster's dictionary
2. Website: http://en.wikipedia.org/wiki/The_God_Delusion
3. Website: http://en.wikipedia.org/wiki/God_Is_Not_Great#Critical_reception
4. Barnes Notes on the Bible Commentary
5. Website: http://www.ucg.org/booklet/bible-true/bible-and-science/
6. Matthew Henry's Commentary

Chapter 2—The Nature of God

1. A.W Tozer, excerpt from *The Knowledge of the Holy*, Authentic Media, 2008, pg. 108
2. Matthew Henry's Commentary
3. Website: http://www.learner.org/resources/series105.html/exploringthepowerofmusic
4. Strong's #4352
5. Jack Frost, *Spiritual Slavery to Spiritual Sonship*, Destiny Image, 2006, pg. 43
6. Ibid 1, pg. 101
7. Clarke's Commentary on the Bible
8. Barnes Notes

Chapter 3—The Mercy of God

1. Website: http://www.sermonillustrator.org
2. The Reader's Digest Encyclopedic Dictionary
3. Strong's #3107
4. Excerpt from Millard J Erickson, *Introducing Christian Doctrine* (second edition), Baker Book House, Grand Rapids, 2001
5. Barnes Notes
6. Millard J Erickson
7. Ibid
8. Ibid 5

Chapter 4—The Goodness of God

1. Ibid chapter 3, 1
2. Webster's dictionary
3. Website: http://www.pbministries.org/books/pink/Attributes/attrib_11.htm
4. Ibid 1
5. See books: Bill Weise, *23 Minutes in Hell*, Chrisma House, 2006 and Mary K Baxter, *A Divine Revelation of Hell*, Whitaker House, 1993
6. Website: http://bible.org/seriespage/goodness-god
7. Ibid
8. Barnes Notes

Chapter 5—The Grace of God

1. Ibid chapter 3, 1
2. Webster's dictionary
3. Website: http://en.wikipedia.org/wiki/John_Newton
4. Strong's #5485
5. Excerpt from Bill Johnson, *When Heaven Invades Earth*, Destiny Image, 2003, pg.   26
6. Barnes Notes
7. Ibid
8. Website: http://www.telegraph.co.uk/travel/8723144/Holiday-hell-From-paradise-to-prison-cell.html

Chapter 6—The Love of God

1. Ibid chapter 3, 1
2. Excerpt from A. W Tozer, *The Knowledge of the Holy*, Authentic Media, 2008, pg. 130
3. Gill's Exposition of the Bible
4. Website: http://www.bibleleague.org/
5. Matthew Henry's Commentary
6. Website: http://www.christiananswers.net/q-abr/abr-a007.html

Chapter 7—The Peace of God

1. Ibid chapter 3, 1
2. Ibid
3. Strong's #1515
4. Matthew Henry's Commentary
5. Gill's Exposition of the Bible
6. Ibid
7. Ibid
8. Ibid
9. Ibid 4
10. Gill's Exposition of the Bible
11. Website: http://www.cacgm.org/youth/most-worry-is-unnecessary.html

Chapter 8—The Faithfulness of God

1. Ibid chapter 3, 1
2. Strong's #530
3. Clarke's Commentary on the Bible
4. Barnes Notes
5. Ibid
6. Excerpt from Ed Cole, *Strong Men in Tough Times*, Water Colour Books, 2003, pg. 73
7. Matthew Henry's Commentary
8. Ibid

Chapter 9—The Abundance of God

1. Mike Murdock, excerpt from *31 Reasons People do not Receive their Financial Harvest*, The Wisdom Centre, 1997, pgs. 62-63.
2. Strong's #4166
3. People's New Testament Commentary
4. Gill's Exposition of the Bible
5. Excerpt from Phil Pringle, *Dead for Nothing?* Pax Ministries, 2000, pgs. 59-60
6. Ibid 1, pg 125
7. Website: http://www.pastoralhelps.com/where-your-treasure-is/
8. Matthew Henry's Commentary

ABOUT THE AUTHOR

Hugh has grown up on the Northern Beaches in Sydney all his life. After completing High School he did a Bachelor of Business in Hotel Management at Southern Cross University. After a year travelling he later did an Advanced Diploma in Christian Ministry and Theology at C3 Oxford Church, Sydney. He has done extensive travelling overseas with family in the UK and USA. Hugh enjoys reading, exercise, all things Rugby League, quality coffee and being involved in his local church.

To write to him, simply email to hughbarber28@gmail.com

Check out his blog at http://faithhopeandreflections.blogspot.com/

Lightning Source UK Ltd.
Milton Keynes UK
UKHW04f0623250918
329480UK00001B/383/P